CRUEL and UNUSUAL IDIOTS

OTHER BOOKS BY LELAND GREGORY

What's the Number for 911?

What's the Number for 911 Again?

The Stupid Crook Book

Hey, Idiot!

Idiots at Work

Bush-Whacked

Idiots in Love

Am-Bushed!

Stupid History

Idiots in Charge

CRUEL and UNUSUAL IDIOTS

Chronicles of MEANNESS and STUPIDITY

LELAND GREGORY

Andrews McMeel
Publishing, LLC

Kansas City

ISBN-13: 978-0-7407-7110-1
ISBN-10: 0-7407-7110-8

Library of Congress Control Number: 2007933998

08 09 10 11 12 RR2 10 9 8 7 6 5 4 3 2 1

Book design by Holly Camerlinck

www.andrewsmcmeel.com

Attention: Schools and Businesses

Andrews McMeel books are available at quantity discounts
with bulk purchase for educational, business, or sales
promotional use. For information, please write to:
Special Sales Department, Andrews McMeel Publishing, LLC,
4520 Main Street, Kansas City, Missouri 64111.

To my wife, Gloria G. Gregory.
We've survived several cruel and unusual events together
and after twenty-nine years there's no one
I would rather go through this life with than you.

A SHORT FUSE

For reasons unknown, Kaleb E. Spangler duct-taped a large "mortar-style" explosive onto a football helmet, placed it on his head, got into a car with some friends, and then lit the fuse. According to an August 16, 2006, story in the *Herald-Times* of Bloomington, Indiana, the massive explosion injured Spangler and, believe it or not, alcohol was involved.

"MAN ACCUSED OF BITING GIRLFRIEND'S SNAKE"

Associated Press headline, August 24, 2007

HAIR TODAY—GONE TOMORROW

In May 2006, Shee Theng, of Edmonton, Alberta, Canada, was sentenced to nine months' community service for partially scalping his then girlfriend. Theng told the judge that the scalping was an accident as he was merely trying to "style" her hair with a power drill. He convinced the judge that he had learned about the barbaric barbering technique from a TV infomercial. Theng admitted he'd known it was a bad idea, because he had screwed up his own hair with the same drill a bit earlier.

A forty-seven-year-old Milwaukee man was arrested for aggravated assault in June 2006, according to the police report, for stabbing a fifty-four-year-old man during an argument about not wanting to have an argument.

L'ART POOR L'ART

In January 2006, artist Trevor Corneliusien told sheriff's deputies that, while camping in California's Mojave Desert, he had shackled his ankles together to be able to draw a picture of his legs. After he had finished his sketch, he realized he didn't have the key to the lock, and had to hop around the desert for nearly twelve hours before finding his way to a gas station. Corneliusien suffered for his art—now it's our turn.

"The man shouted 'God will save me, if he exists,' lowered himself by a rope into the enclosure, took his shoes off, and went up to the lions," stated a zoo official in Kiev, Ukraine, about a June 4, 2006, incident. Thinking it was dinner and a show, "a lioness went straight for him," the official continued, "knocked him down, and severed his carotid artery."

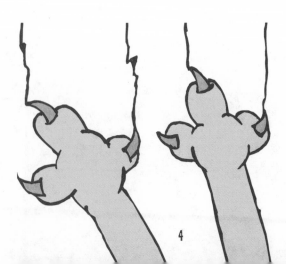

IN THIRTY MINUTES OR LESS

When police pulled over William Bethel on April 27, 2006, because his car didn't have an inspection sticker, they discovered he was also driving on a suspended license. They informed Bethel that they were going to impound his car and, during a routine check of the vehicle, noticed a stretcher, some old clothes, and several pizzas. Bethel told the officers that he not only used the car to deliver Domino's pizzas but also to transport dead bodies to a local funeral home. According to an article in the *Bucks County Courier Times*, Bethel was not arrested and only faced $400 in fines for driving on a suspended license and not having an inspection certificate—as using the same vehicle to transport dinner and the dearly departed is not a violation of county ordinances.

"POLICE TASER MAN WITH CHICKEN IN CAR"

Associated Press headline, September 18, 2007

FATHER'S DAY SURPRISE

Filed in the "How to Really Screw Up Your Kids" category is the case of Shellie White of Arizona. After a custody battle with her ex-husband, White fled the state with her two children and began disguising herself as a man. As reported in a March 28, 2006, Associated Press article, White was arrested in Roanoke Rapids, North Carolina, and confessed that she had convinced her children, ages six and eight, that she was actually their father. I don't think even Hallmark has a card for this.

In January 2006, a nurse from Kyoto, Japan,
was sentenced to more than three years in prison
after she was found guilty of a bizarre way to relieve
work-related stress—tearing off the fingernails
and toenails of incapacitated patients.

MENTALLY DERAILED

Police in Brisbane, Australia, arrested a woman for dangerous driving after she was discovered on a set of railroad tracks, tailgating a train. The woman, who was driving at night with her daughter, told the officers she had taken a wrong turn, ended up on the tracks, and began ". . . honking her car horn at the train as she followed it for 300 meters before being stuck on the tracks."

Oxnard, California, resident Benny Zavala was convicted of animal abuse on October 25, 2002, for killing and dissecting his daughter's pet guinea pig because he believed the rodent was a government spy robot.

TRUNK IN A TRUNK

On May 5, 2004, a fisherman found a portion of the dismembered body of William T. McGuire of Woodbridge, New Jersey, stuffed into a suitcase that had washed ashore of Chesapeake Bay. Over the next several days, two additional suitcases with the rest of Mr. McGuire turned up. (This is one of the rare instances where late luggage wasn't the fault of an airline.) Police confiscated the computer of McGuire's wife, Melanie, a nurse, and discovered she had previously Googled such phrases as "how to commit murder," "instant poisons," "undetectable poisons," as well as researched gun laws. It took the jury thirteen hours to find her guilty of murder, desecration of human remains, perjury, and weapons charges, making this open-and-shut case of three suitcases a brief case.

CRUEL and UNUSUAL IDIOTS

DOESN'T HAVE A LEG TO STAND ON

Police spotted Pasco County, Florida's most notorious traffic violator, Michael Francis Wiley, on May 8, 2007 and gave chase. Wiley, who has been pulled over and either cited or arrested at least 45 times since 1984, and had his license suspended or revoked at least 19 times, was able to evade the cops but they knew who he was. This wily driver had already spent more than three years in prison for various charges, including habitually driving without a license and kicking a state trooper. The last charge makes this story most interesting as the speeding, hard-kicking criminal is a triple amputee (no arms and only one leg).

Rodger Martin, an automotive shop teacher
at Lufkin High School in Texas, was acquitted of
assault charges for smearing habanero pepper sauce
on the face of eighteen-year-old student
Johnathan Glick. The boy claimed Martin had rubbed
the pepper juice on him after Glick had refused
to do the same to a classmate.

Source: KXAN (Austin, Texas), February 21, 2003

GUNS DON'T KILL . . .

Warren County deputies were called to investigate a shooting in Lake Luzerne, New York, on the evening of May 12, 2007. When they arrived, they found the victim, Damion Mosher, had sustained a wound in his abdomen from a .22-caliber bullet. Even though the deputies weren't from the vice squad, they quickly discovered that the perpetrator was . . . a vise. Mosher had been discharging the bullets by clamping them in a steel vise, putting a screwdriver on the primer, and striking the screwdriver with a hammer so he could sell the brass shell casings for scrap (which goes for $1.70 a pound). Mosher was on his nearly hundredth bullet when he lost the final round to a round.

CRUEL *and* UNUSUAL IDIOTS

Richard Stengel was charged with aggravated battery in Ocala, Florida, in December 2001 after he ran over a seventy-seven-year-old woman who was reserving a handicapped parking space by standing in it. Stengel allegedly yelled, "Lady, if you don't move, I'm going to run you over." Then he did.

Source: *St. Petersburg (FL) Times*, March 14, 2002

SONGS IN THE KEY OF B-FLAT

A proud performer is usually the one to utter the old showbiz saying, "I really killed them tonight." But at a karaoke bar in San Mateo, Rizal, Philippines, singer Romy Baligula was singing so off-key that the bar's security officer, Robilito Ortega, pulled his .38-caliber service revolver and shot Baligula in the chest, killing him instantly. The June 2, 2007, incident brings to mind another old showbiz saying about an unappreciative audience, "It's a tough room."

The name of the ninety-year-old man
arrested on July 18, 2007, for public indecency:

Leonard Dickman.

BRIDGE OVER TROUBLED WATER

According to an article in the *Bangor (ME) Daily News*, rescue crews fished an unnamed man out of the Penobscot River after he had jumped off a bridge. The nighttime rescue in June 2007 saved the man's life. "He ended up staving up his face a little bit and doing some bodily injury, but he's okay," a rescue official said. When questioned about the leap, the fifty-two-year-old man told authorities it hadn't been an accident or a suicide attempt, but that he jumped off the bridge because he had "always wanted to." Putting a face on a mother's standard rebuke, "If your friends jumped off a bridge, would you do that, too?"

Christopher Campbell from Cedar Crest, New Mexico, was arrested and charged with cruelty to animals, for the mutilation of his house cats. Campbell claimed the animals were actually supernatural entities that had merely taken the shape of friendly felines.

Source: KRQE-TV (Albuquerque), November 8, 2002

BABY, YOU CAN DRIVE MY CAR

A Pevely, Missouri, woman allowed her baby to go from diaper rash to road rash when she let the baby take the wheel: "She . . . sat the baby on her lap and allowed her to steer while the mother worked the gas and brakes," said police captain Dave Kaltenbronn. The baby and mother weren't injured when their car careered across the centerline and hit an oncoming pickup truck, but the two occupants of the truck suffered several broken bones. When Kaltenbronn questioned the woman about her designated driver, a June 20, 2007, *Festus News Democrat Journal* article quoted him as saying, "She said she let the baby drive because she 'felt it in her heart.'" I'm sure after that accident, more than just the baby's diaper needed changing.

CRUEL AND UNUSUAL (But True) NEWSPAPER HEADLINES

Volume I

"PETS: TO COOK, OR NOT"

Birmingham (AL) News headline, June 8, 2007

"SHOOTING REPORTED AT FIRING RANGE"

The state newspaper of Columbia, South Carolina, headline, August 4, 2006

"POLICE SAY MAN SANG, WIELDED HATCHET DURING ROBBERY ATTEMPT"

headline *Hagerstown (MD) Herald-Mail*, January 4, 2005

"GRISLY MEXICO FACTORY BREEDS MAN-EATING FLIES"

Reuters headline, February 21, 2003

"BLOOD SPRAYS OUT OF SEWER, ON CITY WORKER"

WCCO.com (Minneapolis, MN) headline, March 30, 2007

THAT REALLY BURNS MY . . .

People in Tauranga, New Zealand, reported that they saw a semi-naked man speeding down the road with his butt on fire. John Sullivan ended up in court on February 17, 2003, and was sentenced to two hundred hours of community work for driving an unlicensed motorized barstool. Strategically placing a rolled-up newspaper and lighting it had caused the flames, Sullivan admitted. He also stated that the motorized barstool could reach speeds of up to 50 mph and, on the night in question, he'd "had a few" at the bar before roaring off into the dark. Sullivan's party trick gives a new dimension to the term *tail pipe*.

CRUEL *and* UNUSUAL IDIOTS

A college student in Johnson, Vermont,
became angry with her writing professor
after she was given a poor grade on an essay
that was required for her graduation.
She allegedly threw a pair of cow eyeballs
at him. The student's essay was on the
horrors of slaughterhouses.

Source: *Burlington Free Press*, June 7, 2001

MAKE LOVE NOT WAR

Mr. War N. Marion (not Warren Marion but War N. Marion) stabbed one of his roommates to death and was subsequently charged and found guilty of murder. Even though he admitted to the stabbing, Marion was confused by the man's death because, he stated, he purposely avoided the man's heart and stabbed him on the left side of the chest "to slow him down and calm him down." Marion pleaded guilty to the reduced charge of second-degree reckless homicide while using a dangerous weapon and was sentenced to twenty years in prison. Which hopefully will slow him down and calm him down, too.

Source: *Milwaukee Journal Sentinel*, February 14, 2001;
and *State of Wisconsin v. War N. Marion* (January 18, 2006).

Kevin French of Elmira, New York,
pleaded guilty to shooting his neighbor
in the head using a BB rifle
because the neighbor habitually
mowed his own lawn.

Source: Associated Press, April 29, 2003

NOT REALLY A HANDY MAN

In October 2002, Keith Sanderson, a machine operator at a kitchen worktop factory near Newcastle, in northeastern England, lost part of his right thumb in a workplace accident. Then, five months later, on March 19, 2003, Sanderson wanted to show his boss how the accident occurred and replicated the event almost exactly—except this time he cut off a piece of a finger on his left hand.

CRUEL and UNUSUAL IDIOTS

A twenty-year-old student from
Carleton University in Ottawa, Ontario, Canada,
was engaged in a spitting contest with some
of his friends in April 2004. To project
his spittle the farthest, the young man backed up
and took a running start toward the balcony . . .
and fell eleven floors to his death.

AHEAD OF SCHEDULE

According to an article in the April 22, 2003, edition of the Russian newspaper *Pravda*, a group of Russian train conductors came up with a unique contest as a way of whiling away the hours during their three-thousand-mile journey from Novosibirsk, in Siberia, to Vladivostok. Did they arm wrestle? No. Did they see who could belch the loudest? No. Did they see who had the strongest forehead by smashing it repeatedly against a train window? Yes. The contest was a tie, as they were forced to stop midway through their journey to seek medical attention. I wonder if they were competing over the title of "head conductor."

William W. Bresler Jr. was arrested for
attempted robbery of a National City Bank
in Westerville, Ohio, but instead of being taken
to jail, he was taken in for a psychiatric evaluation—
Bresler had demanded the teller hand over
exactly one penny.

Source: *Westerville News*, March 19, 2003

BEHIND THE TIMES

Anyone with a teenager will know how difficult it is to get an adolescent out of bed in the morning especially if he or she needs to go to school or to work. But one North Port, Florida, woman, Sara Hazeltine, created a cutting-edge way to get her lazy boy hopping—she stuck him in the butt with a knife. "It was dark and I threw a couple of things in the room, not realizing I had picked up a knife," she said. But her nineteen-year-old son claimed his mother took the twelve-inch knife from a wall display and deliberately stabbed him with it. An April 22, 2003, Associated Press article reported that Hazeltine was charged with aggravated assault; her son was treated and released and then moved in with relatives. I guess he finally got the point.

"TEEN STABS STEPFATHER AFTER ARGUMENT OVER THE FAMILY DOG"

WFTV.com (Orlando, FL) headline, September 6, 2007

A FREUDIAN SLIP

A very superstitious twenty-six-year-old man was caught shoplifting from a store in Luocheng, China, and officers strip-searched him, according to an April 25, 2003, report from Ananova. When officers got the man down to his underwear they realized he was wearing women's lingerie. The man hadn't stolen the lingerie, mind you, he wore it, he claimed, because he believed wearing women's underwear would make his crimes undetectable. I suppose he thought "giving someone the slip" meant he should actually wear one.

A twelve-year-old Rockville, Maryland, girl's confession,
which was introduced as evidence at a hearing,
was that she had fatally stabbed her fifteen-year-old
brother during an argument concerning
who could use the phone next.

Source: *Washington Post*, May 21, 2003

TOPPING OFF

"**G**assed" is a slang term for being drunk; except in the case of a thirty-year-old Ethiopian man who was arrested at a gas station in Halle, Germany, for drinking from one of the pumps. "He opted for unleaded and drank 0.14 litres," said police spokeswoman Ulrike Diener. "He paid for the petrol, so he isn't facing any charges." Ananova reported on September 22, 2003, that the man, who not surprisingly was already drunk, was taken to a local hospital for observation but gave no word as to whether he had opted for the car wash or not.

CRUEL *and* UNUSUAL IDIOTS

A forty-seven-year-old man in Aptos, California,
died after he lost his balance while removing
his pants, hopped over to a window
on the second story of his home,
and accidentally fell out.

Source: *Sacramento Bee,* August 2, 2002

A Rose
by Any Other Name …

∼ PART I ∼

Arrested for public urination in Bowling Green, Ohio:
Mr. Joshua Pees.

Bowling Green Sentinel-Tribune, September 5, 2001

• • •

Charged with possession of 33 pounds
of cocaine in Roseville, Michigan:
Denise Coke.

Associated Press, May 5, 2005

• • •

Arrested for robbery in Ottawa, Ontario:
Mr. Emmanuel Innocent.

Ottawa Sun, November 29, 2001

• • •

Police officer **Tracy Sixkiller** arrested
Russell Hogshooter and **Belinda Chewey**
after a police chase in Jay, Oklahoma.

Tulsa World, July 2, 2000

HAM AD HOC

A Ralphs supermarket in Livermore, California, offered a free ham to anyone buying $50 or more worth of groceries. But when Rachael Cheroti saw her total rang up to only $48, she threw a fit and demanded the ham anyway. According to police reports cited in the April 11, 2001, edition of the *San Francisco Chronicle*, the manager acquiesced and gave her the ham. But Cheroti wasn't satisfied and demanded more hams on the premise that she spent so much money at the store every month that she deserved them. The manager rebuffed her assertion and refused to hand over any more hams. Cheroti then rammed the manager with her shopping cart, pinned him against a wall, and wrestled him to the ground. When police arrived, she ham-handedly wrestled one officer to the ground, as well, but was eventually arrested.

A FOOL FOR A CLIENT

Steven McDonald served as his own lawyer during his arson trial in Mount Vernon, Washington, and, while cross-examining himself, he would pose the question as "McDonald the lawyer" and then answer as "McDonald the accused arsonist." According to a February 7, 2002, article in the *Skagit Valley Herald*, to refute earlier testimony from a key police witness who had stated that McDonald was seen at the crime scene "arguing with himself" the accused arsonist knew he needed to directly question himself. "Mr. McDonald," McDonald the lawyer asked, "have you ever talked to yourself?"

"MAN WITH EAR ACHE GETS VASECTOMY"

Reuters headline, August 20, 2003

AN OLD FLAME

An eighty-year-old, while recovering from hip surgery, accidentally ignited the fumes from an old tank he was removing and suffered burns over 40 percent of his body. The man, who ironically enough lives in Burnaby, British Columbia, put out the flames, went inside his house, cut off his burned clothes and hair, took a cold bath to cool down and applied skin lotion to his burns—and then decided to call an ambulance. The October 3, 2003, Reuters article reported that the man had a reputation for being "tough as nails" and was outside dressed and waiting for the ambulance when it arrived. Police said the man was recovering at a local hospital "in good spirits, laughing, talking and blaming the incident on his stupidity."

According to a May 21, 2003, news report on Philadelphia, Pennsylvania's NBC10.com, a thirty-eight-year-old man from Pine Creek Valley, Delaware, suffered burns to his head and arms when he attempted to dispose of gunpowder by tossing it onto the burning logs in his fireplace.

GET A GRIP

According to a January 8, 2004, article in the *South China Morning Post*, a twenty-one-year-old waiter cut off three fingers to win back the heart of his beloved, Xiao Qian. Qian called police to have her former lover removed from outside her home and, while the officers were leading him away, he decided to subtract a few digits. Although her ex only wanted Qian's ring finger she gave him the middle one by not visiting him in the hospital.

"CANDLES RECALLED BECAUSE OF FLAME RISK"

Associated Press headline, March 28, 2005

I'LL KEEP AN EYE OUT FOR YOU

The ever-watchful eye of a surveillance camera or closed-circuit television has helped catch many a thief while plying his or her trade. When fifty antique glass eyes went missing on Christmas Eve 2003 from the Owensboro Medical Health System in Kentucky, a security videotape quickly helped identify the criminal. However, police were baffled over why someone would steal glass eyes, as there isn't a high demand for them on the black market. But the most unusual fact about this crime is the suspect's name. Are you ready? The person arrested for stealing fifty glass eyes was—Melissa Jane Wink.

Kenneth Ware allegedly stabbed his brother to death
in Brooklyn, New York, because he wouldn't return
Kenneth's New York Yankees cap.

Source: *New York Post*, July 12, 2003

WHO PUT THE NUT IN DOUGHNUT?

Houston, Texas, ambulance driver Larry A. Wesley was suspended in July 2000 because, while transporting an injured child to the Ben Taub Hospital, he stopped to get doughnuts and juice. Wesley filed an unlawful discrimination lawsuit claiming intentional infliction of emotional distress. He stated that had he been a white man, he wouldn't have been disciplined so seriously. According to an article in the July 13, 2007, *Houston Chronicle*, it was a piece of cake for a federal judge to throw Wesley's case out of court. The doughnut-eating EMS driver was left with a glazed look in his eyes.

"I've warned you bastards
many times about
leaving my mailbox open,
now you will pay."

From a letter written by Lexington, Kentucky, resident George Krushinski, who was charged with planting small incendiary devices in a mailbox and a postal vehicle because a postman, working the weekend route, habitually left Krushinski's mailbox door open.

Source: *Lexington Herald-Leader*, November 16, 2002

AN UNSTABLE RELATIONSHIP

A Scottish transsexual called 999 (Scotland's version of 911) screaming, "I'm being murdered," and then something about a little hoarse—even though the operator could hear her clearly. What the caller, Kaye Campbell, was referring to wasn't a case of laryngitis but an actual little horse, a Shetland pony Kaye and her wife kept in their bathroom. Kaye was cleaning up hoofprints in the bathroom when her wife, Joanne, went on a rampage about their little pony, threw a knife at Kaye, seized her hair, repeatedly hit her head against a fireplace, and struck her with a pot stand. According to a December 12, 2002, article in the *Daily Record* (Glasgow), Kaye quickly hoofed it out of their home after Joanne's unstable attack. When questioned, Joanne, not wanting to be saddled with charges of aggressive horseplay, denied everything.

"SON DECAPITATES MOTHER WITH CIRCULAR SAW, DIES TRYING TO CUT OFF HIS OWN HEAD"

USA Today headline, May 9, 2007

HOOK, LINE, AND STINKER

We've all heard that fish is brain food, but one Cape Town, South African man could do well eating more fish as opposed to throwing them. The *Cape Times* reported on November 21, 2002, about the man's odd habit of throwing rotten fish at people in their cars, train passengers, and even congregants of a local church. Police didn't arrest the man as his activities weren't considered serious and they hoped he would voluntarily scale back on his fish-flinging fetish.

Sheila Raven Lord, a forty-nine-year-old woman
from Glenview, Illinois, allegedly stabbed a
male companion with a steak knife because
he was humming a Megadeth song so loudly,
she couldn't hear the Celine Dion song
to which she was trying to listen.

Source: *Edgebrook-Sauganash Times Review*, November 7, 2002

THAT'S A MORAY

Some people are crazy about their pets and some people's idea of what constitutes a pet is crazy. In 1969, Paul Richter brought home his catch from a day of fishing at the local canal in Bochum, Germany, and gave it to his wife, Hannelore, to cook. But when the kids saw what was in the pot, they wanted to keep it in the tub—the bathtub; and that's where Aalfred the eel has lived ever since. But, according to BBC News from February 4, 2003, animal rights activists thought keeping Aalfred (*aal* is the German word for "eel") in a tub was eel-treating him and demanded he be released. However, Aalfred was allowed to stay with the Richter family after a local veterinarian gave him a clean gill of health.

"STUDENT MAY BE SUSPENDED FOR STRANGLING HIS TEACHER"

Star (Malaysia) headline, July 28, 2007

ANOTHER BRICK IN THE WALL

The *Merced (CA) Sun-Star* reported on December 10, 2002, that police were called to investigate an incident involving an unnamed man who was taken to a Modesto, California, hospital after his head was split open by a brick. Eyewitnesses quickly made it clear to investigators that the victim was the one who was actually as thick as a brick. Apparently he had tossed the brick into the air at 2:30 A.M. to see how high he could throw it and, as it was dark, lost sight of it until it came back down to strike him. Obviously, the guy was a real blockhead.

CRUEL *and* UNUSUAL IDIOTS

Police in Los Angeles speculated that a twenty-one-year-old man deliberately parked his car, with his girlfriend inside, on a set of train tracks as a train was approaching. The man jumped out of the car moments before impact. Even though the train obliterated the car, the woman survived. The car literally exploded into hundreds of sharp pieces of flying shrapnel, and it was this debris that struck and killed the man as he was running from the scene.

Source: *Los Angeles Times*, May 22, 2007

CRUEL AND UNUSUAL (But True) NEWSPAPER HEADLINES

Volume II

"Crematory Consumed by Fire"

Chattanooga (TN) Times Free Press headline, May 5, 2007

///

"Woman with No Baby Given Caesarean"

Herald Sun (Melbourne, Australia) headline, September 11, 2003

///

"Man Gets Life Sentence for Spitting"

Tulsa World headline, May 22, 2003

///

"Man Dies after Head-butt by Armless Man"

Associated Press headline, September 18, 2007

///

"Man Killed in Argument during Scrabble Game"

New Zealand Herald, July 15, 2006

LOCK, STOCK, AND BARREL

The Associated Press reported on January 24, 2003, that Raymond Poore Jr. called his wife at work from their Winchester, Virginia, home and told her that the dog had bitten him and he intended to kill it. When she arrived home, she discovered blood and dog hair on the broken stock of a shotgun and the smell of gunpowder in the air. She then saw her unconscious husband bloodied from scratches, dog bites, and a gaping hole in his chest. Police surmised that Raymond had been pummeling the couple's thirty-pound shar pei with the butt of the loaded shotgun when the weapon discharged—frightening the dog and killing its owner.

The name of the thirty-eight-year-old woman charged on June 11, 2007, with stealing toilet paper from the Marshalltown, Iowa, courthouse:

Suzanne Butts.

REACH OUT AND TOUCH SOMEONE

When police spotted Olga Esquivel Ramirez, of St. Peter, Minnesota, driving erratically, they turned on their sirens and took chase—but Ramirez didn't slow down. She continued driving for four miles until, according to the *St. Peter Herald* of August 30, 2001, she was finally pinned in by several cruisers. When confronted, Ramirez claimed she wasn't trying to elude the officers. She told them that she thought if they really wanted her to pull over they would just call her on her cell phone. If she keeps up this behavior, the next phone she'll be using will be a different kind of cell phone.

Louis Dethy, a retired Belgian engineer,
was embroiled in a feud with his ex-wife and
their fourteen children. Dethy rigged nineteen
deadly booby traps throughout his home near
Charlerois so as to hurt anyone who attempted to
take ownership of the house. He must have forgotten
the location of one of the traps because
he was killed after accidentally setting it off.

Source: *National Post–Sunday Telegraph* (London), November 11, 2002

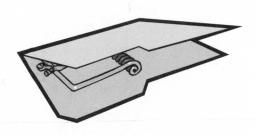

FOWL ACTS OF TERRORISM

L arry Ray Pratt was the first person in Johnson County, Kansas, charged under a new food-supply protection law (the Bioterrorism Act of 2002). He was arrested after employees of the Dillons Store identified his photograph in a lineup. He was convicted of criminal trespass and criminal damage to property, both misdemeanors. He was sentenced to ten days in jail and a year on probation. An article in the July 11, 2003, *Topeka Capital-Journal* reported that Pratt's act of bioterrorism consisted of his urinating on packages of chicken in a supermarket cooler. Pratt now belongs to a long line of terrorists who are considered yellow-bellied chickens.

"Look at this!"

The classic final words from a thirty-two-year-old man from Santa Cruz, California, who wanted his friends to see him dangling precariously from a hotel balcony— moments before he fell to his death.

Source: *Santa Cruz Sentinel*, October 5, 2002

SCAVENGER HUNT

Police in West Vancouver, British Columbia, Canada, arrested multimillionaire Eugene Mah and his son, Avery, on charges of theft. But we're not talking about a white collar/Enron-type crime, we're talking about petty theft. The rich father-and-son team (worth an estimated $13 million) stole hundreds of items from their upscale neighborhood, including garbage cans, concrete lawn decorations, and even government recycling boxes that they stored in their own elegant home. According to an article in the April 26, 2001, edition of the *Canadian Press*, the Mahs also stole their neighbor's welcome mat—and every one of the fourteen welcome mats that indefatigable family purchased as replacements.

CRUEL *and* UNUSUAL IDIOTS

WARNING: CONTENTS UNDER PRESSURE

On February 17, 2003, Leonia, New Jersey, resident Selimy Mensah was hospitalized with second- and third-degree burns to her face and hands after a fire broke out in her apartment. According to police, the fire started when Mensah tried to open a can of aerosol spray paint with an electric can opener.

Emmanuel Nieves was charged with
aggravated assault by police in
Mansfield Township and Hackettstown,
New Jersey, after slashing the face of his friend,
Erik Saporito, following an argument they had
over which one had the hairiest butt.

Source: *Easton (PA) Express-Times*, November 15, 2002

TOUGH AND RUTHLESS–
ROUGH AND TOOTHLESS

Jason Morris was accused of the vicious crime of taking a pair of pliers and yanking out eighteen of his girlfriend's teeth, leaving her in agonizing pain and covered in her own blood. During the trial in Greater Manchester, England, according to a November 23, 2002, article in the *Guardian*, the jury acquitted Morris of all charges after his girlfriend, Samantha Court, confessed to having extracted the teeth herself. She admitted she had pulled her own teeth during a drug binge in an attempt to get rid of a hallucinated green and pink fly that had flown down her throat. Court confided to the jury that, after her dental debacle, she and Morris had decided to stop doing drugs.

CRUEL *and* UNUSUAL IDIOTS

Chad Landreth of Samsula, Florida,
was accused of shooting a truck driver to death
because the man parked his truck over
Landreth's septic tank and wouldn't move it.

Source: *Orlando Sentinel*, June 15, 2003

THE OTHER MAGIC BULLET

A workplace brawl in Irvine, California, quickly turned fatal when one man grabbed another in a headlock and put a gun to his head. It was reported in August 2000 that the man fired the gun, shooting his victim in the face—but the victim wasn't the one who died. The bullet passed through the man's cheek and lodged deep into the shooter's own chest—killing him. This guy went from giving a headlock to getting a headstone.

"WOMAN STABS BOYFRIEND IN THE EYE WITH CHOPSTICK— 6 YEARS AFTER SHE BLINDED THE OTHER EYE WITH HER FINGER"

Reuters headline, July 5, 2007

UNLEADED AND LEADED

Marc Fowler was arrested by members of the Capital Area Regional Fugitive Task Force (United States Marshal's Service and Metropolitan Police Department) on November 20, 2006, and charged with the January 31, 2003, murder of Allen Price. Price was shot in the head at a Hess gas station in the Washington, D.C., area, with the entire incident being captured by a surveillance camera. One of the most disturbing elements of this crime, apart from the actual murder, is the tape showing people walking around Mr. Price's bleeding body and one indifferent customer who stared at the corpse, finished pumping his gas, and then simply drove off.

"RESTAURANT SERVES FOOD IN TOILET BOWLS"

Associated Press headline, June 3, 2005

RUMM-SHPRINGA

A drag race on a country road south of Fort Wayne, Indiana, took a bad turn when one of the drivers lost control and caused a head-on collision, leaving one woman with a head injury. According to an April 14, 2003, *Indianapolis Star* article, what makes this story unique is that the drag race was between two Amish horse-drawn buggies. The driver of a third buggy, David Wickey, was arrested on charges of driving while intoxicated.

Clayton Frank Stoker, a Johnson County, Texas,
corrections officer, was charged with
first-degree murder for shooting
Johnny Joslin on July 28, 2002.
Stoker and Joslin had been out bar-hopping
with two other men when they got into
an argument over which one of them would
go to heaven and which would go to hell.

TWO, TWO TWAINS

A young woman in Hamlin, West Virginia, needed to make a call on her cell phone and decided to follow safe-driving guidelines by pulling off the road. Unfortunately, the area of the road in which she chose to pull off, according to the January 8, 2003, *Lincoln Journal*, was already occupied by two sets of train tracks. Before her call was connected, an oncoming train connected with her car, flinging it onto the other set of tracks. The woman's train of thought was again put off track when another train, traveling in the other direction, smashed into her car. Surprisingly, the woman survived both train collisions.

Weeks after a man collapsed and died during a meeting of the Milwaukee, Wisconsin, chapter of Alcoholics Anonymous, his identity was still a mystery as people attending meetings usually do so anonymously.

Source: *St. Louis Post-Dispatch*, June 3, 2001

REMAINS OF THE DAY

Larry Bennett had spent his life savings on medical expenses because of ongoing health problems (he had been on life support three times and had several strokes) and was considered indigent by the state. Because of his health, his ex-wife, Brenda Pitts Bennett, had allowed Larry to continue living in her house even though they had been divorced for ten years. When Larry died on February 26, 2005, Brenda received $1,000 from the state, which she thought would cover Larry's embalming and burial expenses, but it didn't. The funeral home "made us pick Larry's body up or they would send him to lost and found," she told the *Dallas Morning News* on March 18, 2005. Not knowing what to do with his body, Brenda left it in her SUV parked in her driveway for two days while she tried to make arrangements.

LET THEM EAT CAKE

A woman described as "rather large" took offense, on August 19, 2003, when a customer at a Top Food store in Kent, Washington, leaned past her to ask a supermarket employee when a new batch of Zingers snack cakes would arrive. "Don't you talk around me," said the thirty-four-year-old, who then began whacking the would-be snacker on the head. A manager trying to break up the confrontation was met with a barrage of Twinkies, Ding Dongs, Ho Ho's, Snoballs, Suzy Q's, and other cakes. Police who arrived on the scene sustained several injuries from the escalating food fight before arresting the goodies pitcher. This might be the case for a lawyer to once again try the "Twinkie Defense."

"MAN BLAMES CRASH ON IMAGINARY FRIEND"

Hartland (WI) Lake Country Reporter headline, January 30, 2005

WHERE THE BOYS ARE

A twelve-year-old boy and one of his friends were caught vandalizing stop signs in the Avon Park, Florida, neighborhood, causing more than a thousand dollars' damage. The boys weren't acting alone, according to an April 15, 2003, *Highlands Today* article. Police arrested April Marie Brown, the mother of one of the boys, who had willingly chauffeured them around in her car during their Saturday night vandalism spree.

A twenty-four-year-old Cedar City, Utah, man
was given a citation for littering
after he allegedly shaved his head
and flung the hair clippings over a fence
into his neighbor's yard.

Source: *Salt Lake Tribune*, September 10, 2002

ON THE ROAD

The *Denver Post* reported on September 2, 2003, that a twenty-year-old man was killed during afternoon rush hour when he leapt from a car going about 40 mph. According to the victim's friends, the man had been planning on jumping for a while, but not to kill himself—he thought enduring the pain would give him the courage to get a tattoo. Unfortunately, the only ink the man got was a small blurb in the news section and then again in the obituary column.

CRUEL and UNUSUAL IDIOTS

Eldon, Oklahoma, resident Pearl Lynne Smith allegedly shot her husband to death during an altercation as to who was responsible for feeding the couple's goats.

Source: Reuters, June 12, 2003

HE'S MAKING A LIST
AND CHECKING IT TWICE

"**A** bottle comes flying through her door and immediately lights up her living room," said Hermosa Beach police sergeant Paul Wolcott. "She was barely able to escape with her life." Wolcott was describing the aftermath of a Molotov cocktail thrown through a woman's glass front door, causing $200,000 in damages. Brandi Nicole Nason threw the gasoline bomb on Christmas Day 2003 into the home of her former stepmother because Nason was dissatisfied with a Christmas gift the woman had given her.

CRUEL *and* UNUSUAL IDIOTS

A neighbor's house in Osaka, Japan, was blocking the view Hiroshi Nishizaki so treasured. In a plot to get the neighbor to move, Nishizaki poured urine on the offending house on 169 occasions before he was caught. He is accused of causing damage to the house in the amount of $5,500.

Source: *Mainichi Daily News* (Japan), May 18, 2007

A STICKY STICKUP

A gang of six gunmen raided a Bromor Foods warehouse near Johannesburg, South Africa, and used masking tape to tie up, blindfold, and gag security guards. When the guards finally managed to free themselves, they discovered that the robbers had gotten away with twenty-one pallets of . . . chewing gum. An estimated $14,000 worth of Chappies chewing gum was reported as stolen on January 22, 2004. Authorities are impressed that the thieves could steal and chew gum at the same time.

According to a police investigation cited in a June 1, 2007, report on Orlando, Florida's WKMG-TV, a burglar attempted to break into the Maranatha Used Clothing store in Miami by crawling between the blades of a massive ventilation fan. Before squeezing completely through the fan blades, he accidentally kicked the electrical connection that started the fan.

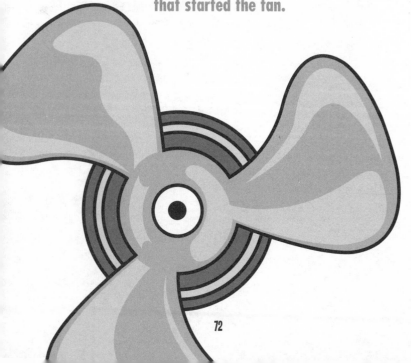

INNOCENT BY REASON OF GUILT

In some cases, a defense lawyer won't let their client testify as the person might unwittingly incriminate him- and herself. But fifteen minutes after Charles Douglas Stephens Jr. took the stand, his sworn testimony convinced the jury he was innocent of the charge of robbing a convenience store. The *St. Petersburg (FL) Times* reported on March 22, 2001, that Stephens, who had served time for murder, stated that if circumstances warranted, he would kill again. But, he said, he definitely wasn't the person responsible for robbing a Circle K because he wouldn't be "so stupid" as to leave any witnesses alive. He was acquitted of all charges because if you can't trust the words of a convicted killer, who can you trust?

Toni Lynn Lycan was tired of her downstairs neighbor's habit of playing music at full blast, so she retaliated by forcefully stomping up and down on the floor. Apparently, her stomping became too forceful and the Vancouver, Washington, woman was taken to the hospital after she broke both her legs about four inches below the knee.

Source: *Columbian*, October 17, 2003

SMOKING IS DANGEROUS TO YOUR HEALTH

Cleburne, Texas, residents Mr. and Mrs. David Pawlik were curious to see "blue flames" flare up every time Mrs. Pawlik lit a cigarette, so David called the fire department to see if it was something with which they should be concerned. An inspector told Pawlik not to light another cigarette, flick the lighter, or strike a match until he came over to investigate. Unfortunately, Mrs. Pawlik became nervous about having her house inspected and instinctively lit a cigarette to calm her nerves. According to a July 11, 2007, article in the *Fort Worth Star-Telegram*, the subsequent explosion killed her instantly. Investigators discovered that the Pawlik house was not connected to the city gas line—however, a natural gas leak underneath their yard had slowly filled their home with gas.

"15 INJURED IN KITE CONTESTS"

Independent Television (Great Britain) headline, January 16, 2003

LAYING IT ON PRETTY THICK

"When I approached the van I could smell the stench 20 to 30 feet away," Texas Department of Public Safety trooper Jim Cleland told the *Palestine Herald-Press* in its February 5, 2004, edition. "It was then I discovered the animals." What Trooper Cleland found was twenty-three dogs, three cats, and a chicken in a van. Animal feces were piled one foot deep in sections, and the driver and her elderly passenger were covered in the same stinky substance. Robin Vanwert was arrested on suspicion of drunken driving, which I guess was obvious because she was already sh*t faced.

A SWAT team was finally able to swoop in and capture a thirty-six-year-old man after a ten-hour standoff at a hotel in Houston, Texas. The ordeal first began when the man threatened to kill hotel workers because there was no ice.

Source: *Houston Chronicle*, September 20, 2003

MEAT MY BOYFRIEND

When a jilted boyfriend wants revenge, there's no telling what he might do—and in the case of Liam McGarry of Scotland, there was no telling why he did what he did; in fact, he didn't even know. McGarry turned up at the home of Laura Barr, who had broken off their relationship a month earlier. She said McGarry didn't even look like himself—mainly because he was covered in minced (ground) meat. A neighbor came over to help remove McGarry after he had slapped Barr and spat chunks of meat in her face. An article in the March 13, 2004, edition of the *Daily Record* reported McGarry's defense lawyer as saying, "He is at a complete loss to explain the significance of the mince or why he had coated himself in it."

"NO CHARGES IN CASE OF MANNEQUIN SALESMAN CAUGHT BOILING SKULLS IN HIS APARTMENT"

USA Today headline, May 3, 2007

HITTING THE NAIL ON THE HEAD

While having a few beers with his friends, Brad Shorten, an Australian handyman, started joking about construction site accidents. He picked up his nail gun as a visual aid and accidentally shot himself in the head. Reuters reported on March 7, 2004, that Brad (the man) shot a brad (the nail) fully into his brain, leaving only a small red dot on his temple. A team of specialists performed a risky four-hour operation in which part of the skull was removed to extract the 1.25-inch nail. Doctors commented that had the nail gone one centimeter deeper, it could have caused permanent brain damage, a stroke, or paralysis. So basically, it was lucky that Brad Shorten got the short end of the brad.

Bedford, Kentucky, resident Danny Ginn
was arrested after calling 911 to say he had
hijacked a garbage truck and was holding it hostage—
in retaliation for the truck driver's persistently
using Ginn's driveway to turn around.

Source: *Madison (IN) Courier*, August 6, 2003

... AND HE SHOWS THEM PEARLY WHITE

After snorkeling off Caves Beach, north of Sydney, Australia, Luke Tresoglavic swam one thousand feet to shore, walked to his car, and drove to the local surf club to show everyone the shark he had brought with him. Lifeguards were stunned by the creature, not because of its size but because it was attached to Tresoglavic's leg and wouldn't let go. They forced fresh water into the gills of the two-foot-long carpet shark and that eventually released its grip. Tresoglavic told the Australian Broadcasting Corporation (ABC) radio on February 11, 2004, that he was fine and didn't even require stitches, only a course of antibiotics. The shark didn't make it. Tresoglavic reportedly buried it in his garden—I guess that's what happens when you become attached to an animal.

MY LIPS ARE SEALED

Airport security has tightened significantly since 9/11 and it's difficult to get anything through screening—especially if it's the severed head of a harbor seal. A man who claimed to be a biology professor, flying from Boston's Logan International Airport to Denver, asserted that he had found a dead seal on Revere Beach and cut off its head for educational use. The Associated Press reported on March 22, 2004, that the man was permitted to board the aircraft—but the seal's head was confiscated. Supermodel Heidi Klum threatened legal action until she discovered the head the man had cut off belonged to a harbor seal—not her husband, Seal.

CRUEL and UNUSUAL IDIOTS

Twenty-year-old Judith Ann Garland of
Baltimore, Maryland, was arrested
for offering to sell a two-year-old boy
because she had been arrested on drug charges
and needed $250 for bail.

Source: *Baltimore Sun*, September 3, 2003

SCREW THE POOCH

Little Rock, Arkansas, television station KATV reported on December 9, 2003, about an eighteen-year-old man who thought his pit bull was too old and docile and decided to kill it. The teenager, Eugene Weston Jr., and his cousin took the dog to an abandoned cotton gin outside the city limits of Eudora, and planned to drown the dog in a filthy pit filled with water, oil, diesel fuel, and hydraulic fluid. But before they could put the pit bull in the pit, Weston lost his balance, fell in, and couldn't get out. The cousin ran to call 911 while Weston's father, Eugene Weston Sr., jumped into the pit to save his son. Both father and son drowned in the accident—the pit bull, however, survived the ordeal unscathed.

CRUEL *and* UNUSUAL IDIOTS

A thirty-seven-year-old
Council Bluffs, Iowa, man, Jay Glaspey,
was hospitalized after he burst into flames
while trying to set fire to his girlfriend's bed
after a fight.

Source: *Daily Nonpareil*–Associated Press, September 23, 2002

A Rose
by Any Other Name ...

～ PART II ～

Escaped from the same Saskatoon, Saskatchewan,
prison three times:
Mr. Richard Slippery.

National Post (Canada), October 6, 2001

• • •

Pleaded guilty to manslaughter in Pierre, South Dakota:
Mr. Austin First In Trouble.

Sioux Falls Argus Leader, August 24, 2006

• • •

Escaped from the Montana State Hospital for the
mentally ill in Warm Springs:
Mr. Terry Crazy.

Associated Press, May 26, 2001

• • •

A planning commissioner charged with lewd behavior
toward a child in Clover, South Carolina:
Mr. Rusty Cockman.

Rock Hill Herald, October 21, 2000

REMOVE ORIGINAL FROM GLASS

In the hustle and bustle that was the first-floor lobby of the Saint Louis County Courthouse, Daniel F. Everett felt an overwhelming need to make copies as he knew he was a little behind. So, he quickly pulled down his pants, jumped up on the machine's glass surface, and began making copies of his behind. The January 12, 2001, edition of the *St. Louis Post-Dispatch* related that Everett had made two copies (possibly one of each cheek) and was working on a third when Clayton, Missouri, police officers arrested him for disturbing the peace. Eyewitness accounts claimed Everett was uncertain why he was being forced to tone down his behavior and pleaded with the officers, yelling, "What did I do? What did I do?"

CRUEL *and* UNUSUAL IDIOTS

A nineteen-year-old man was scheduled for trial for allegedly shooting another man at a concert in retaliation for the victim's having given him a "wedgie."

Source: Associated Press, August 23, 2002

A REAL HOTHEAD

Thomas Woods and his roommate, Rod Bennett, had been drinking heavily when Woods challenged Bennett to a test of endurance. Before Bennett knew what was happening, Woods set fire to a rug in their Davis Park, New York, house, and threw down the gauntlet—"Let's see which one of us leaves first." Bennett decided to forfeit the challenge and ran out of the house after Woods took out his pre–World War I Mauser pistol and fired off a few rounds. Bennett went to a neighbor's house and asked him to call 911, according to an April 18, 2004, article in *Newsday*. Even though the fire was quickly contained, Woods never made it out. So by losing his life, Woods actually won the dare.

"HUMAN CANNONBALL FIRED OVER HIS FEAR OF FLYING"

Times (London) headline, June 16, 2005

A REAL DEVIATED SEPTUM

A man with the most incongruent name, Angel Jones of Toronto, Canada, was convicted of aggravated assault against his girlfriend on February 17, 2002. Jones, who had been paroled the day of the attack, was picked up at the jail by his girlfriend. She then cooked him a meal and the two made love. Jones became enraged and accused his girlfriend of being unfaithful because of some new sexual techniques she tried while they were in bed. He grabbed her roughly and then . . . bit off her nose. Jones admitted that the nose was in his mouth but claimed, "Her nose just popped off as she pulled her head back" and that, because of her weight-loss medication, the organ had become brittle and "just fell off."

U.S. Army veteran Erik Beelman was shot to death by U.S. Marine veteran Christopher Marlowe in New Orleans following an argument over which branch of the military is tougher.

Source: *Times-Picayune*, June 28, 2006

FOLLOW THE DIRECTIONS
IN THE ORDER LISTED

According to an August 4, 2004, Associated Press article, the double murder of Carl and Sarah Collier was prompted by their insistence that their granddaughter, fifteen-year-old Holly Harvey, stop doing drugs and end her lesbian relationship with sixteen-year-old Sally Ketchum. When police apprehended the two teenagers on suspicion of murder, the evidence against them was pretty convincing: three bloody knives, a truck with traces of the elderly couple's blood, the testimony of friends from whom the girls allegedly tried to obtain guns, and a to-do list written on Harvey's arm, reading, "Kill, keys, money, jewelry." But she forgot one other item: jail.

CRUEL *and* UNUSUAL IDIOTS

In an effort to claim his fifteen minutes of fame,
a seventeen-year-old boy climbed over a handrail
in California's Mount Diablo State Park to fake a fall
so his buddies could capture it on film and post it
on MySpace. His pals got more than they bargained for
when their friend lost his balance, fell about
seventy-five feet onto some jagged rocks,
and was seriously injured.

Source: *San Jose Mercury News*, June 12, 2007

SEE YA LATER . . .

What's the difference between an alligator and a crocodile? Most people would answer that an alligator has a wide U-shaped, rounded snout, whereas a crocodile has a longer, more pointed V-shaped nose. But David Havenner of Port Orange, Florida, would say the difference between the two is that an alligator is something you can use to hit your girlfriend. Havenner was arrested after throwing beer cans at Nancy Monico and then slapping her with a live three-foot alligator he kept in their mobile home. Havenner said he resorted to this reptilian behavior, according to a July 17, 2004, Associated Press article, because Monico angrily bit his hand when she discovered there was no beer left in the trailer.

"ALLIGATOR EATS COCKER SPANIEL"

Tampa Tribune headline, October 10, 2005

A MAN OF THE ENLIGHTENMENT

Celebrating the Fourth of July with fireworks is an American tradition—especially if your name is Thomas Jefferson. The Thomas Jefferson in this story isn't the fiery redheaded president of the United States—but he was fiery. The so-named Indiana teen and a few of his friends were shooting off fireworks on July 4, 2004, when they ran out of things to blow up—so they decided to set fire to one another's clothes instead. Jefferson suffered severe burns after he doused his shirt with gasoline and another boy set him on fire. Even though it wasn't the smartest thing he's ever done—it was certainly the brightest.

"Shoot me, you *^#@! (you don't have) the guts!"

the last words spoken by a nineteen-year-old Albuquerque, New Mexico, man who was lethally shot in the forehead by his seventeen-year-old brother.

Source: *Albuquerque Journal*, September 27, 2002

HE AIN'T NO HANK HILL

In November 1998, a thirty-three-year-old man fired up his blowtorch and set about cutting up a fifty-five-gallon steel drum to sell it for scrap metal. What the Ascutney, Vermont, man didn't realize was that the drum contained propane. What he did realize, very quickly, is that propane is highly explosive—a lesson he learned the week before when he caused an identical explosion from an identical drum of propane. The first time, he had merely blown off his mask, the second time, he, well, let's just say the second time was his last time.

Pablo Castro was involved in a real case of double jeopardy when he was admitted to the same Decatur, Alabama, hospital twice in one day (June 24, 2007). He had been stabbed in an argument, treated, and released, then got into another argument with a different person and was stabbed again.

Source: *Decatur Daily*, June 26, 2007

REALLY STICKING HIS NECK OUT

We've all heard the expression "gallows humor," but the men who operate the gallows in Kuala Lumpur, Malaysia, haven't found the humor in the last three hangings. That's because, between 1998 and 2000, three executioners have accidentally killed themselves while clowning around on the job. The last hangman, while preparing for an upcoming execution, wanted a photograph of himself on the gallows with a noose around his neck when, as reported on November 29, 2000, the trapdoor gave way, instantly breaking his neck. Which only proved that he both did and didn't know what he was doing.

"SQUIRREL FIRES REGULAR OCCURRENCE IN CANADIAN BORDER TOWN"

Associated Press headline, July 19, 2005

THUMBTHING'S WRONG

Charles Gibson of Lakeland, Florida, asked Charles Smith to give him a haircut but, when he looked into Smith's eyes, he knew the man wasn't cut out for the job. "He looked all hyped up like he was high," said Gibson. "I told him, 'That's OK, I'll get my hair cut by somebody else.' That's when he revolted." Smith demanded the $5 for the haircut and when Gibson refused, the two began fighting. Smith pulled a straight razor from his barber kit but Gibson grabbed his hand. Smith then leaned over and bit off Gibson's thumb. "Then he spit it out and escaped," Gibson recalled of the December 2005 event. Smith was charged with aggravated battery and, unfortunately, doctors were unable to reattach Gibson's right thumb.

OPEN WIDE AND SAY "AHHHHHHHH!!!!!!"

You'll really hate going to the dentist after you hear about Theodoros Vassiliadis, who termed his dental techniques as "pioneering" but which his patients termed "torture." In Athens, Greece, Vassiliadis was sentenced to four years in prison thanks to the testimony of seven former patients, in July 2005. "The screws he put in were thirty millimeters [1.2 inches] long," claimed patient Sofia Grigoriadis. Others who testified had suffered similarly from oversized screws that, in some cases, pierced their sinus cavity and were allegedly taken from Vassiliadis's television set. Hopefully, now that he's in jail, Vassiliadis is the one getting drilled.

"IT'S NATIONAL HAIRBALL AWARENESS DAY"

Philadelphia Inquirer headline, April 28, 2006

CRUEL and UNUSUAL IDIOTS

HEAVE HO!

An article in the September 15, 2001, edition of Tokyo's *Mainichi Daily News* reported that a twenty-five-year-old bulimic woman from Toyoda (near Nagoya) was arrested for excessive violations of the country's Waste Disposal Act. Police identified the woman, although they didn't release her name, as being the notorious vomit dumper—responsible for discarding nearly sixty pounds of vomit per week for a year. When questioned by the police concerning her activity the woman responded, "I didn't want to throw away the vomit near my home, so I took it to faraway places." She had to walk to the dump to dispose of her puke because she couldn't hurl it that far.

Steven Deere was sitting down to a breakfast
of eggs and leftover pork with the rest of his family
when his stepson demanded fresh bacon
instead of leftovers. Deere didn't take the demand
very lightly and shot the younger man
with a 9 mm pistol.

Source: *Pittsburgh Tribune-Review*, December 27, 2002

WHAT'S THIS ALL ABOUT, THEN?

"I don't know what the motive was for this crime, but it's definitely unacceptable," said Constable Jacqueline Chaput of Winnipeg, Manitoba, Canada. What wasn't acceptable in the constable's eyes was an unprovoked attack on a wheelchair-bound man at a church in the Centennial neighborhood of central Winnipeg. The man was assaulted, yanked out of his wheelchair, thrown down a flight of stairs, and pelted with concrete paving stones. On September 27, 2007, the Canadian Broadcasting Corporation (CBC) News reported that the stones were thrown at the man from a height of six to ten feet, and that he "did sustain some fairly serious injuries to his facial area and his head." I can't believe the irony of an assailant being the first one to cast stones at a church.

CLEANUP ON AISLE NINE!

Twenty-three-year-old Pablo Lopez Jarquin was shot, execution style, in the back of the head, in a convenience store in Santa Cruz, California, while a surveillance camera captured the entire event. "Pretty callous" is how police sergeant Steve Clark described it—but he wasn't talking about the murder in Rosy's Market & Taqueria. He was referring to other customers in the store who continued shopping while the victim lay bleeding on the floor. According to a May 31, 2002, Associated Press article, several customers even went so far as to step over the dying man to bring their purchases to the counter.

"MAN SAYS TIGHT JEANS CAUSED AGGRAVATED ASSAULT CHARGE"

USA Today headline, December 1, 2004

THEY'RE HERE ALREADY! YOU'RE NEXT!

In a follow-up story conducted by ABC News and the Associated Press on October 9, 2002, Gary Damon Stephens freely admitted to the murder of his parents five years earlier. Stephens also maintained that his earlier rationale is still valid—the people he killed weren't his real parents, they were actually pod people posing as his parents.

CRUEL and UNUSUAL IDIOTS

Mr. Bonney Eberendu was sentenced to a mental health facility by a judge in London's Southwark Crown Court after Eberendu confessed in court to smearing his feces inside at least six trains over a period of several months.
In his defense Eberendu said that, on at least five occasions, he had been ordered by voices in his head to murder somebody—but he was able to override that desire by wiping his poop on things while riding the rails.

Source: *Metro* (London), June 11, 2007

ONE DOWN, NINE TO GO

Giving a politician the finger is a traditional form of protest—but usually it's only a temporary gesture. But one Japanese man, Yoshihiro Tanjo, was so angry that Prime Minister Shinzo Abe didn't visit a Shinto war shrine on the anniversary of Japan's surrender that ended World War II that he literally gave him the finger—his little finger, to be exact. Tanjo was arrested and charged with intimidation after chopping off and mailing his left pinky finger, along with a DVD showing the self-imposed amputation, to Abe on August 16, 2007, the day after the sixty-second anniversary of the Imperial Rescript on the Termination of the War. Tanjo was a day late and a finger short.

Jeffrey Lee Daniels of Barstow, California,
admitted to accepting $10 from a
fifty-eight-year-old male acquaintance for
the opportunity to sleep in the same bed with him.
But Daniel said he was shocked and incensed when
the man touched him "in the area of his butt"
and he wound up killing the man.

Source: *Victorville Daily Press*, December 5, 2002

NO PLACE TO PUT YOUR HAT

A thief, or thieves, broke into a funeral home in Toronto, Canada, and stole something very personal from one of the corpses—its head. The family of sixty-eight-year-old Cecile Lemay demanded the return of their mother's head that was removed on July 10, 2005. The thieves weren't completely heartless as they left the dead woman's earrings and a cash donation. The April 26, 2006, edition of the *Globe and Mail* quoted Lemay's sister, Carmelle, as saying, "Each morning, when we get up, we ask ourselves: 'Where is the head? Will it show up on our lawn one morning?'" As a heads-up, the family has offered a reward of nearly $10,000 dollars for the head's safe return.

"PSYCHIC'S CRYSTAL BALL BURNS DOWN HIS FLAT IN UNFORESEEN BLAZE"

Times (London) headline, August 12, 2005

WHAT ALES YA?

Police discovered that what caused the death of an elderly Saint Louis man was a Stag. The Stag in question was not the animal, not the party, but the beer. Corine Jones, sixty-six, admitted to shooting her seventy-one-year-old husband, Robert, four to five times in the chest because he gave her a warm Stag. Corine was charged with first-degree murder and armed criminal action for the December 3, 2006, shooting. Talk about "opening up a six-pack of whoop-ass" on someone.

CRUEL and UNUSUAL IDIOTS

James Coldwell went out on a limb in July 2007 and robbed a Citizens Bank branch in Manchester, New Hampshire, disguised as a tree. Coldwell was identified from images on the security camera even though he had duct-taped branches to his body and head, and leaves covered most of his face.

Source: *Washington Post*, July 8, 2007

SHOPPING AROUND FOR TROUBLE

Gardenia Zakrzewski Johansson pulled into the parking lot of the Neiman Marcus store in Scottsdale, Arizona, and gave the valet the keys to her BMW. Before she and her little dog went into the store, she asked the valet if he could keep an eye on something she'd left in the backseat—her two-year-old son. According to the December 12, 2006, *Mesa East Valley Tribune*, when Johansson emerged from the store thirty minutes later, with a full shopping bag, police were there to bag her. Johansson confessed she didn't know the name of the valet to whom she had given her keys but did remember he had brown hair. She apologized for taking so long in the store but, she explained, her Christmas present wasn't wrapped, she needed to stop and get some cosmetics, and then she met an old friend and had a chat. It was then Johansson's turn to ride in the backseat—of a squad car.

WHERE THERE'S A WILL, THERE'S A FRAY

Sarah Zabolotny, twenty-nine, was in the courthouse in Buckhannon, West Virginia, in March 2006 to take care of a speeding ticket. She was apprehended shortly after leaving the building. Was she caught speeding again? No, she was caught stealing something from the courthouse and was accosted by a court clerk before the police arrived. Zabolotny asked the clerk if she could just give back the item but he said no. So what trinket did Zabolotny steal? She was seen on a surveillance camera folding up an eight-foot rug before weaving out of the building.

"VACUUMING MAN SHOOTS HIMSELF"

St. Cloud (MN) Times headline, April 11, 2005

ATTENTION, WAL-MART SHOPPERS!!!

According to an article in the July 11, 2006, *Globe and Mail/Canadian Press*, a Wal-Mart in St.-Jean-sur-Richelieu, Quebec, Canada, received a bomb threat and quickly evacuated its customers. It turned out to be a false alarm, which was very lucky for the store's forty employees, because they were ordered to search through the store to locate the bomb. Had there actually been a bomb that detonated, the store would have gone from a red-tag sale to a toe-tag sale.

Willie Tarpley of Brandon, Florida, was arrested for allegedly killing his ex-wife's boyfriend because the man was a registered sex offender. However, both Tarpley and his ex-wife are also registered sex offenders.

Source: United Press International, May 14, 2007

CAUTION: OPEN WITH CARE

A man in his workshop on the outskirts of Rio de Janeiro, Brazil, found a rocket-propelled grenade and did the only sensible thing—he tried opening it with a sledgehammer. Reuters reported on August 9, 2006, that the man apparently was trying to recover scrap metal from the grenade but, after the explosion, neighbors were busy trying to find the scraps of the man.

CRUEL and UNUSUAL IDIOTS

An eighteen-year-old Mongolian girl was taken to a Beijing hospital to undergo medical test after eating dirt for eleven years. According to a May 2006 report on China Central Television, the young girl's habit started when she was seven, when she discovered that her favorite dirt dish was yellow mud. Neighbors complained to the girl's family as she had been caught several times dining on their mud-thatched roof.

¡YO QUIERO TACO BELL!

After making several thousand "runs for the border" a dozen masked men were seen hauling six forty-gallon trash bags filled with Taco Bell sauce packets back to a store on South Western Avenue in Marion, Indiana. The *Chronicle Tribune* reported on September 10, 2006, that in addition to the estimated twenty-five thousand packets, there was a note explaining that the packets had been collected for a considerable amount of time and that it was decided to return them to their rightful owners. A Taco Bell representative said the company hands out about six billion sauce packets a year—which is barely enough to make the food tolerable.

Police were looking for Raul Ponce Jr.; they suspected he was responsible for the murder of his girlfriend, who had been stabbed 122 times. Ponce was tracked to and arrested while he was attending his anger-management class.

Source: *San Diego Union-Tribune*, June 23, 2007

CRUEL *and* UNUSUAL
IDIOTS

(But True)

CRUEL AND UNUSUAL ∧ NEWSPAPER HEADLINES

Volume III

"Jordanian Kills Sister over Mobile Phone Photo"

Agence France-Presse, April 25, 2005

"Man Authorities Say Killed after Taco Argument Convicted"

Associated Press headline, August 21, 2007

"Argument over Beer, Spaghetti Leads to AK-47 Shooting"

WFTV.com headline, Orlando, Florida, November 29, 2005

"Deodorant Row Led to Stabbing"

Oxford Mail headline, June 3, 1998

"Police: Argument over Remote May Have Led to Double Murder"

Associated Press headline, September 18, 2007

PULLING THE WOOL OVER HIS EYES

A man from the southern Nigerian village of Isseluku was arrested for murdering his brother with an ax—but the man claimed a kid had tricked him. The kid he was referring to was a young goat that stubbornly wouldn't leave his farm. According to a September 17, 2006, Associated Press article, the man claimed that he had become angry after the animal got his goat and he'd struck it with an ax—it was then that the goat miraculously turned into his dead brother.

Christopher Chamberlain, who became upset when Jamie Davidson, his ex-girlfriend, told his underage drinking buddies to leave, grabbed the leash of Davidson's mother's poodle, and whipped the dog against the deck, the side of the house, and Sharon's head—bruising the woman's head and breaking the dog's neck. He told police Davidson was "just mad because I killed her [expletive] dog."

Source: *Boston Herald*, February 12, 2002

CRUEL *and* UNUSUAL IDIOTS

✳

BUS DRIVER—MOVE THAT BUS!!!

In the show *Extreme Makeover: Home Edition*, a group of designers descend on a house and transform it while the owners are away—and that's sort of what happened to one Cool, California, residence. Terence Michael Dean was arrested for breaking and entering and making some bold design choices. He had left all the faucets running, arranged packages of meat in the bathtub and sink, crafted a shrine of Buddha on a bongo drum, scattered a trail of potting soil from a walkway to the shrine, put teddy bears in three plant stands, dug up nearly one hundred plants in the yard, and left a piece of paper floating in a cup of water with the sentence "I love Cherry" written on it. The homeowner said, in the September 24, 2006, edition of the *Mountain Democrat* newspaper, that when he arrived home he saw Dean escape clothed only in a sheet.

DOWN IN THE MOUTH

This story will make you clench your jaw and other parts of your body, as well. According to the *Daily Telegraph* (London), in an article from January 13, 2007, dentist David Quelch was found guilty by the British General Dental Council of serious professional misconduct. The council ruled that Quelch could no longer practice dentistry, after he pulled two teeth out of an eighty-seven-year-old patient against her will, without anesthesia, because she had complained about previous treatments. He was quoted as saying, "That'll teach you not to complain . . ."

"PSYCHOLOGISTS DISSECT THE MULTIPLE MEANINGS OF MEOW"

Cox News Service headline, May 30, 2003

BIID THEM FAREWELL

Body integrity identity disorder (BIID), also known as amputee identity disorder, is a psychiatric disorder that gives one the overwhelming desire to amputate one or more healthy limbs or other parts of the body. What? You've never heard of it? It's all the rage, you know. A recent case involved a woman using the pseudonym "Susan Smith," who wrote a first-person essay titled "I Won't Be Happy until I Lose My Legs," published in the January 29, 2007, edition of the *Guardian* (Manchester). "The image I have of myself has always been one without legs," said Smith. The worst part was freezing her leg in dry ice for nearly four hours to kill it—because surgeons cannot legally or ethically amputate a healthy appendage. She plans on having her second leg removed in the future—at least she's goal oriented.

A CHILLING DISCOVERY

Murfreesboro, Tennessee, police raided the home of William Davis after complaints from neighbors. They found what they were looking for in several freezers: not money or drugs but 114 dead cats and one dead dog. Davis filed a $1.5 million lawsuit against the city because he said the icy critters had "emotional value" for him. In his petition, made public by TheSmokingGun.com on January 5, 2007, Davis also claimed he had plans to create his own pet cemetery and therefore the animals were considered "business property." In addition, one of the 114 frozen felines, he stated, was certain to wind up in the *Guinness Book of World Records* because of its enormous size at birth. My question is, why only one dog?

"GERMAN POLICE RESCUE 91-YEAR-OLD MAN GLUED TO ROOF"

Reuters headline, March 13, 2007

POSTER CHILDREN

Two student organizations, the Islami Jamiat-e-Talba (IJT) and Pakhtoon Students Federation (PSF) from the Dawood Engineering College in Karachi, Pakistan, got into a fight over which group would put up a particular poster first. Six students were injured in the January 27, 2007, fight. The message on the poster that started the brawl urged students not to fight on campus.

The Reverend Robert Nichols, who has been teaching anger-management classes for several years in Gary, Indiana, was arrested and charged with beating his wife.

Source: Associated Press, July 24, 2007

BLADE RUNNER II

The *Connecticut Post* reported on March 5, 2007, about Fermin Rodriguez from Bridgeport, who was charged with assault after brutally stabbing his wife multiple times following an argument over suspected infidelity. Police statements claimed that after Rodriguez was finished stabbing his wife, he gave the knife to the couple's two-year-old son and said, "Now, you stab Mommy." I know one child who's going to need a lot of therapy when he's older.

Charles Flowers, the director of the very strict Christian camp, Love Demonstrated Ministries, was arrested for dragging a fifteen-year-old camp attendee behind a van because she wasn't able to or refused to keep pace on a morning run.

Source: *Houston Chronicle*, August 10, 2007

HAIR OF THE DOG

Mr. Mount Lee Lacy (couldn't make up that name if I wanted to) was arrested in his Gainesville, Florida, apartment and charged with animal cruelty, following his girlfriend's mother's request that police intervene. After officers were confronted at the door by Lacy's aggressive mastiff, they noticed a Jack Russell terrier suffering with a bloody paw. According to a police sergeant, when Lacy was questioned about the wounded animal, he said, "Biting the dog was good punishment and that's how you train them, that dogs bite so that's what they understand." A December 14, 2004, article in the *Gainesville Sun* reported that Lacy admitted he routinely bit the dog as part of obedience training.

"UPSET WITH WIFE'S ONLINE CHATS, MAN SHOOTS COMPUTER"

Scranton (PA) Times-Tribune headline, June 14, 2007

SIBLING RIVALRY

An intoxicated Robert Bayley stopped by his brother's Raleigh, North Carolina, home to retrieve a power drill he had earlier loaned James Carroll Bayley. According to a May 3, 2005, article in the *Raleigh News & Observer*, James told police that he felt he needed to protect himself from his brother, so he grabbed his gun. He must have really felt threatened by Robert, as he "shot him in the right leg to knock him down," he told the judge at his sentencing. "Then," said James, "after a short time, I shot him in the head to make him dizzy so he would fall." It made Robert more than dizzy and James pleaded guilty to the charge of murder.

"I couldn't take it anymore."

Principal Maria Pantalone accused of throwing excrement at school kids.

Source: *Toronto Star*, April 2, 2007

CRUEL *and* UNUSUAL IDIOTS

PRIMED AND READY

Michael Lewis, twenty-seven, decided to test his level of marksmanship by shooting a pellet gun at a .22-caliber bullet he saw lying on a picnic table. His accuracy was amazing and he hit the bullet on the primer. To Lewis's delight, the bullet exploded—but to his dismay, fragments of the bullet lodged in his groin. The *Salina Journal* reported on March 28, 2005, that Lewis was taken to a local hospital. Surprisingly, alcohol had not been involved.

CRUEL *and* UNUSUAL IDIOTS

Megan Conroy of Brisbane, Australia, is very particular about the way her first name is pronounced—it's "Mee-gan" not "May-gun." In fact, she is so sensitive that she pleaded guilty to assault after an unidentified forty-year-old man mispronounced it—and she kicked him in the testicles.

Source: *The Age* (Melbourne), September 6, 2007

FOR YOU I'D BLEED MYSELF DRY

"Oh, no, not that song! I can't stand that song!" shouted a woman in the audience at karaoke night at the Changes bar in Seattle, Washington. She couldn't bear another rendition of the Coldplay song "Yellow." According to an article in the August 9, 2007, *Seattle Post-Intelligencer*, she charged the stage screaming and then shoved the man at the microphone—it took four Changes employees to pull the woman off and hold her for police. When the wild woman attacked him, the song wasn't the only thing that was yellow.

"CRASH PLANE WAS BELOW CORRECT HEIGHT"

Associated Press headline, June 3, 2005

YOU SHOULD SEE THEM
RIDE A UNICYCLE

Abbotsford, Wisconsin, police were temporarily confused when they pulled over a 1985 Chevrolet truck for reckless driving and found two Dorchester men in the driver's side (and no, they weren't doing anything nasty). According to a *Marshfield News-Herald* article from August 28, 2007, Havey J. Miller, who has no legs, was steering the truck while Edwin Marzinske was on the floorboard operating the pedals. Both men were issued citations for drunk driving and driving after their licenses had been revoked. A third man from the vehicle, who was also drunk but did have his legs, used them to walk home after the August 18 incident.

"LAW & DISORDER:
WOMAN, 38, CHARGED IN HIT,
HIT, HIT, HIT, HIT, RUN"

Jacksonville (Fla.) Times-Union headline, December 21, 2006

BIRDS OF A FEATHER

"It started out as a physical confrontation, but it escalated until both of them were shooting at each other," Detective Sergeant A. D. Beasley of the Mercer County (West Virginia) Sheriff's Department said about a father and son who played a unique game of chicken. According to police, a gun battle broke out between Jackie Lee Shrader and his twenty-four-year-old son, Harley Lee, over the best way to cook skinless chicken. The argument started before a Sunday dinner on September 19, 2004, and ended with both men firing .22-caliber handguns at each other and the younger Shrader catching a bullet to the head. Harley was taken to a local hospital, treated, and released—he was, after all, only shot in the head.

Ramon Cabrera was sentenced to ninety-nine years
in prison for killing David Saenz, a street musician,
because the victim did not know Cabrera's favorite song,
"El Guajolote" (The Turkey).

Source: Reuters, March 10, 2001

DIDN'T YOU LEARN ANYTHING FROM THE MOVIE *PSYCHO*?

An illegal immigrant from Honduras, Solomon Rodriguez, was arrested on September 20, 2004, for the death of a forty-nine-year-old San Antonio man. An affidavit stated that Rodriguez allegedly stabbed Roy Hernandez multiple times while Hernandez was taking a shower at home. The victim managed to crawl to a neighbor's house for help but died shortly afterward. Rodriguez admitted that earlier in the week, the two had argued over breakfast and two tortillas.

"CHURCHGOER STABS 5 AFTER LISTENING TO SERMON"

Philippine Daily Inquirer headline, July 17, 2007

A FRESH EDUCATION MOVEMENT

A first grade teacher at Dallas's Gabe P. Allen Elementary School was placed on administrative leave after she had a six-year-old student bring home something he had done in class. Dallas school district spokesman Donald Claxton said, "It generally appears the teacher was trying to help raise awareness with the family." According to an article in the September 25, 2004, edition of the *Houston Chronicle*, the teacher refused to take any crap from the young student so, after he made a pooh-pooh on the classroom floor she wrapped it up and stuck it in his backpack along with a note. Maybe the first grader thought the teacher had said, "Use your bowels," not "Use your vowels."

A thirty-five-year-old woman, Catherine Delgado, was arrested in Annapolis, Maryland, after she appeared in a hotel lobby with "large slabs of fudge bulging out of her pockets." In a bit of inspired investigation, a police officer checked a nearby Fudge Kitchen store and discovered the display in the front window was gone and the door to the store was open.

Source: _Washington Post_, August 3, 2007

LURED INTO DANGER

A thirty-one-year-old man from the town of Brazil (near Terre Haute), Indiana, was accidentally killed when a pipe bomb he was carrying exploded. According to an August 6, 2006, news report on WRTV (Indianapolis), the man didn't have the explosive for terrorist activity but was probably going to use it to help him catch fish in Birch Creek. Making *him* the one that got away.

"TWO ACCUSED OF BRINGING STOLEN COFFEE MAKER TO WHITE PLAINS BRAWL"

White Plains Journal News headline, October 6, 2005

A TWO-FISTED BURGER

Joseph Manuel Augusto couldn't have it his way when he wanted to get into the bathroom at a Burger King in Stratford, Connecticut, because Andres Diaz was still using the facilities. The *New Haven Register*'s article about the incident from July 20, 2004, said the two got into a whopper of a fight over Diaz's prolonged potty break. Augusto attacked Diaz with a small pocketknife and Diaz retaliated by beating Augusto with a straw dispenser. A case I like to refer to as "the BM at the BK."

In August 2006, forty-year-old Darrell Rodgers
was treated at Bloomington (Indiana) Hospital for a
self-inflicted gunshot wound to his left knee.
Rogers explained that he had shot himself while seeking
to relieve the pain in his knee; the discomfort
probably stemmed from his shooting himself
in the same knee ten years earlier.

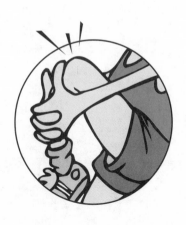

CABIN FEVER

David Mason was on a Braathens airline flight home to
England from Norway when he started thumbing through a
pornographic magazine he had brought aboard. When he came
to a picture of a black man with a white woman, Mason became
outraged and demanded that the flight attendant burn the magazine
in the plane's galley oven. According to the BBC News on
September 21, 2004, the stewardess denied Mason's request and sent
him back to his seat. A few moment's later, passengers complained
of a burning smell and it was discovered that Mason had set fire to
the magazine himself. The crew quickly extinguished the fire and
Mason was arrested when the plane landed.

"SIX SKULLS, A SEVERED HAND AND A STRIPPER"

USA Today headline, July 25, 2006

CAST THE FIRST STONE

Two women in a church in western Germany had an altercation at the altar. One, who had a cold, sneezed throughout the service, and the other's "God bless you" soon became "God something-else you!" After mass, the two got into a fight outside the church. The exasperated churchgoer continued to insult the woman with the cold who simply turned the other cheek—it was, however, the cheeks of her butt that the cold-sufferer turned toward the other woman, when she mooned her. The sneezer received a minor eye injury and the rest of the congregation got an eyeful.

JARRETT WOULD BE DISAPPOINTED

Delvin Nelson was arrested after he threatened to blow up a Subway on December 15, 2004. But not the subway in New York, a Subway sandwich shop in Houston. Nelson, an employee for the city's public works department, got hot under the collar over a cold steak-and-cheese sandwich. Nelson threw the sandwich at the manager and then threatened to kill her and blow up the store. He was arrested for making a terrorist threat and assaulting a sandwich artist.

Mike Harstad of Jamestown, California,
used a can of Pledge and a cigarette lighter in
an attempt to destroy a wasps' nest.
He wound up causing a fire that destroyed his
mobile home, a truck, a boat, a trailer,
and an outbuilding.

Source: KVML-AM (Sonora, CA), July 1, 2007

SMOKE 'EM IF YOU GOT 'EM

"I saw a flash of light and I just jumped up and went in the kitchen. I saw my friend and his beard was on fire," Richard Creech recalled. "It was very shocking." What Creech was referring to was his friend, Henry Laskin, of Pasco Country, Florida, who was trying to light a cigarette from his stove. So how did Laskin catch on fire? He was wearing nasal prongs connected to an oxygen tank and, when the oxygen came in contact with an open flame—well, you do the physics. Laskin was airlifted to Tampa General Hospital following the December 16, 2004, accident. Had the oxygen tank exploded, he wouldn't have needed the plane to get to Tampa.

Michael Schoop tried to convince a judge in
Oakland, California, that the reason he had
child pornography on his computer was that
he had accidentally downloaded the material
while searching the Internet for asparagus recipes.
The judge didn't buy it.

Source: *San Francisco Chronicle*, October 28, 2003

NO MAGIC GENIE, EITHER

"It wasn't bubbling fast enough for him," Claudia Quinn guessed of her son's unusual experiment, "because when we walked in the stove was on at the lowest setting." She was talking about what she found when she and her husband went to check on their son, Philip, in his trailer in Kent, Washington. "There was glass from the kitchen clear to the living room," Claudia told KOMO 4 News on November 29, 2004. "They said it appeared that a piece of glass punctured his heart." The glass came from a lava lamp that exploded when Philip decided to heat it on the stove.

Robert M. Suszynski was arrested in February 2003 in Rochester, New Hampshire, and charged with assault. Suszynski told police he became angry with a man who continued to complain about how much pain he was in after a fire and wanted him to shut up— so he hit him with a baseball bat.

Source: *Boston Herald*, March 1, 2003

CRUEL *and* UNUSUAL
IDIOTS

NOT PART OF THE TEST

In the early morning hours of December 18, 2004, on Route 130 in Bordentown Township (New Jersey), Sergeant Norman Hand pulled over William Grieb for drunk driving. Hand ordered Grieb to perform a field sobriety test. What happened next, according to Hand, was "the kind of stuff you see on TV but can't believe would happen here." Before the allegedly intoxicated Grieb could finish the test, he was run over and killed by an eighteen-wheeler driven by an intoxicated Shane Gildersleeve.

"17 REMAIN DEAD IN MORGUE SHOOTING SPREE"

Raleigh (NC) News & Observer headline, September 4, 2001

I'LL TAKE A SHOT AT IT

Alexander Joseph Swandic of Orofino, Idaho, had obtained what he thought was a bulletproof vest, so he and his friend David John Hueth tested it by shooting at it a few times. Confident that it was indeed a bulletproof vest, Swandic put it on and asked his friend to shoot him. Being the good friend that he was, Hueth obliged and put a hole through the vest and through Swandic, as well. Police arrived at the scene of the shooting and discovered that Swandic hadn't found a bulletproof vest but rather a flak jacket, designed to stop shrapnel and other indirect low-velocity projectiles. Hueth didn't give the police any flack when he was arrested and, according to an Associated Press story of December 16, 2004, charged with involuntary manslaughter.

CRUEL *and* UNUSUAL IDIOTS

A twenty-three-year-old woman and her twenty-seven-year-old companion, both of Ocean Springs, Mississippi, were struck by a car and killed—because they were standing in the left lane of Interstate 10, arguing.

Source: *Biloxi Sun Herald*, June 27, 2006

DOG-DAY AFTERNOON

The Romanian daily newspaper *Ziarul de Iasi* reported on January 10, 2005, that a man "wanted to get rid of the neighbor's dog which was bigger than his and made too much noise at night." So the man injected strychnine into some food, threw it over the fence, and watched as the dog gobbled it down. But nothing happened and this made the Romanian man ever angrier. He then went to see the consumer protection chief to complain—not about the dog but about the poor quality of strychnine he had acquired. The man also filed an official complaint against the poison manufacturers because their product didn't kill his neighbor's dog.

"MAN FACES CHARGES IN SWORD ATTACK OVER PUPPY"

Associated Press headline, September 12, 2007

CRUISING THE MALL

A twenty-year-old man obviously didn't know the difference between the gas and the brake when he drove his car through a fifth-floor wall of a parking garage, reported the *South Florida Sun-Sentinel* on December 14, 2004. The man only suffered minor injuries when his car landed inside the second floor of a store at the Shops of Sunset Place, located in South Miami. I don't think that's what the mall meant by "convenient parking."

Lee Damron, wielding a sword, and
Richard Cavalier, brandishing a 9 mm handgun,
battled over a handicapped parking space in front
of the Oak Hill Hospital in Spring Hill, Florida.
Although he was confined to a wheelchair,
Cavalier got the drop on Damron and
won the coveted space.

Source: *St. Petersburg Times*, March 13, 2002

A REAL BELTING

A ninety-three-year-old man, Joseph Kubic Sr., was rushed to the hospital in Stratford, Connecticut, suffering from a gunshot wound to the neck. Kubic was injured, according to a February 19, 1999, article in the *Connecticut Post*, because he had lost a little weight—he was shot while trying to hammer a pointy-nosed bullet through his belt to make an additional notch. Ultimately, he did make a little notch—just not in the belt.

An eighty-year-old man, whose name was not released by the press, was accidentally killed in Downey, California. The man, whom neighbors said, "hated everybody," was attempting to put an explosive device in a neighbor's home but carelessly set his arm on fire while trying to light it. The fire on his arm ignited the fuse and the bomb exploded, killing him instantly.

Source: Associated Press, January 9, 2006

A SMEAR CAMPAIGN

The driver of an automobile transport trunk told police he thought he had hit the mangled carcass of a deer, reported the *Orlando Sentinel* on September 23, 1999. But why was the deer wearing clothes? Because it wasn't a deer, it was a bicyclist who had been struck by a car and thrown twenty feet onto the Florida Turnpike—and then repeatedly run over by at least six vehicles. "They just kept going," said police detective Norris Butler. "The first two or three had to have known it was a body because of the clothing." The body of the unidentified bicyclist was scattered over 375 feet of highway and only one motorist stopped—because the debris from the bicycle punctured a tire.

CRUEL *and* UNUSUAL
IDIOTS

Walter Travis Jr. of Indianapolis, Indiana,
was arrested for shooting at his neighbor,
Michael Culver, several times with a
.38-caliber revolver after Culver's dachshund,
BJ, allegedly pooped in Travis's yard.

Source: *Montreal Mirror*, August 6, 2003

DADDY DEAREST

In March 2000, a judge in Dedham, Massachusetts, sentenced Thomas Flanagan to nine years in prison for the nearly continuous physical abuse of his wife and three children. Flanagan was indicted on three counts of attempted murder and thirty-nine counts of assault and battery, including what the children referred to as "plucking." Investigators working on Flanagan's case were told by the kids that their father made them line up every day so that he could take a pair of tweezers and pluck out their nose hair. Making Flanagan the winner of the plucking worst father of the year award (or at least a word that rhymes with *plucking*).

"PATROL CAR HIT BY FLYING OUTHOUSE"

Milwaukee Journal Sentinel headline, October 3, 2003

FROM "SEVEN" TO "THIRTY"

During his February 14, 2000, murder trial in France, Pierre Navelot told the court of Metz that, during high school, his professional ambition was to "kill people." Navelot was found guilty and sentenced to thirty years for stabbing a young woman twenty-two times in an attempt to cut off her head—which he wanted to give to his former girlfriend. Navelot said he was inspired to become a world-famous serial killer after seeing the movie *Seven*, but that his career was cut short when he was caught after only one murder. He bragged that he had once written a thirteen-page "career plan" that included the names of about twenty potential victims. "You can't live just being nobody at all," Navelot said—but he proved himself wrong.

CRUEL and UNUSUAL IDIOTS

A forty-nine-year-old Milwaukee, Wisconsin, woman
was angrily trying to get her boyfriend's attention
by flicking lighted matches on him as he lay under
a sheet on the bed. She soon got his attention,
all right, when the bed burst into flames. Her boyfriend
and the five other people living in the house survived
but the flicking femme fatale died as a result
of smoke inhalation.

Source: *Milwaukee Journal Sentinel*, January 23, 2006

THE THREE STOOGES

Thirty-nine-year-old Des Moines, Iowa, resident Pamela Oliver was arrested in April 2000 and charged with assault. But Oliver didn't actually do the assaulting; she persuaded three complete strangers she had met on the street to beat up her husband. The three men surprised Oliver's husband and beat him up as she'd requested, then it was Oliver's time to be surprised when the police arrested her. Oliver said she was shocked to find out that what she did was illegal, especially since she never even offered to pay the three assailants. And some people say that chivalry is dead.

City officials notified David Watts of Apex,
North Carolina, that the eighty sheep he had been
keeping in his home as pets were going to be impounded.
Neighbors had been tolerant of Watts's odd behavior
but, when some of the sheep wandered out of his house
and into a cemetery and ate its fresh floral
arrangements, they filed a complaint.

Source: *Raleigh News & Observer*, March 27, 2007

NO SMOKING—GAS PRESENT

According to a March 22, 2007, story, in the Scottish newspaper *Dunfermline Press*, Stewart Laidlaw, thirty-five, was banished from Thirsty Kirsty's pub in the Royal Burgh of Dunfermline, in the town of Fife, after several customers complained about his noxious emissions. A stunned Laidlaw said no one had complained about his flatulence before, but he did state that a new law could be to blame. On March 26, 2006, Scotland enacted one of the toughest smoking bans in Europe and now, Laidlaw conceded, there was no smoke to cover up the smell.

"MAN SHOOTS FRIEND IN ARGUMENT OVER HEIGHT OF LATE SOUL SINGER JAMES BROWN"

Associated Press headline, January 11, 2007

THIS GUY IS NUTS

Police in Guelph, Ontario, are on the lookout for a Caucasian male in his early twenties with a goatee and a large gap between his front teeth. According to a May 28, 2007, Associated Press article, the man hasn't broken any laws nor has he harmed anyone, but police are "concerned." Six women complained that the man approached them and asked for a unique favor—he wanted each of them to kick him in the groin. According to Sergeant Cate Welsh, "Some of the women obliged him. I would imagine it would be quite painful, but he didn't make a peep, just stood up and went on his way." On two occasions, the man approached on a bicycle—how he pedaled away afterward is anyone's guess.

"It means more than just a hat. It's like my crown.
It's like asking a king to remove his crown."
Twenty-two-year-old Charles Littleton angrily refused
to remove his Los Angeles Dodgers baseball cap
during a Saginaw (Michigan) City Council meeting.
He became defiant after he was asked to either
remove his hat or leave, and was eventually
Tasered by police.

Source: WJRT-TV (Flint, MI), November 13, 2006

HAIR TODAY, GONE TOMORROW

An emergency call was received about an apartment fire in June 2000 in Fargo, North Dakota, and firefighters and police were dispatched. Upon arriving at the apartment, the emergency personnel encountered thick smoke billowing from a window and a stench that one crewmember described as "noxious and terrible." After the door was broken down, firefighters noticed the tenant standing in a corner with his fists raised as if to fight. The man eventually revealed both the cause and the source of the fire: he routinely collects all his cut hair from barber visits and, once a year piles it into a pan and sets it on fire. The man also claimed he worked for the FBI. Nonetheless, he was arrested for threatening the firefighters.

"REWARD OFFERED FOR MISSING KIDNEY"

Seattle (WA) Times headline, January 5, 2007

SHOVEL OR NOTHING

The expression "I can dig it" took on a whole (or hole) new meaning in 2001 when William Lyttle was discovered to have been obsessively digging tunnels underneath his twenty-room house in North London, England. Lyttle burrowed past his property line and a cave-in caused a fifteen-foot hole to open up in the street. Five years later, Lyttle, now in his midseventies, was temporarily removed from his house when it was found that his mole mania had threatened the integrity of the entire street and, combined with the overwhelming amount of junk he had also accumulated, his house was in danger of sinking into the ground.

Claiming that he did it to meet women,
Matthew Damsky, a student at the University of
Central Florida, admitted in June 2006 that he set fire
to a couch in his dorm.

A DRAIN ON OUR SPECIES

Robert Jones of Adel, Georgia, was burned by a drain cleaner that caused, he said, "extensive, excruciating burns and destruction of flesh," so he filed a lawsuit against the company. In an *Atlanta Journal-Constitution* article from June 15, 2000, Jones claimed that had the manufacturer not made the container look so flimsy, he wouldn't have removed the contents. Jones had poured Liquid Fire from its original container into another "safer" container of his own design and it was from that vessel that the cleaner had leaked.

Roger Hunt claimed he and his girlfriend were simply going out on a New Year's Eve dinner date in his truck when he was arrested by police. Hunt was charged with kidnapping in Warren, Ohio, when the officers noticed the girlfriend was barefoot. They didn't buy Hunt's nervous explanation, "She's from Virginia. She doesn't wear shoes [when she goes out to dinner]."

Source: *Warren Tribune-Chronicle*, January 3, 2003

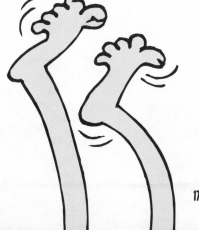

A LONG WAY FROM FARGO

It was must have been both the best and worst day of her life after a young Phoenix, Arizona, woman accepted the second marriage proposal from her twenty-year-old boyfriend. The man, who worked at a landscaping business, asked her if she would go with him to his worksite in August 2000. Once there, he took her hand, led her over to a wood chipper, turned on the machine, and climbed in. Before she knew what was happening, the man, whose hand she had just accepted in holy matrimony, was using that same hand to pull her into the machine. She quickly turned into the runaway bride and escaped, while her fiancé simply went to pieces.

Mao Savoeun, from the Kompong Thom province in central Cambodia, hit the nail on the head when she came up with a way to derail her thirteen-year-old daughter's obsession with partying— she nailed the girl's foot to the floor.

Source: Reuters, November 22, 2002

IT'S IN THE BAG

Ricardo Meana, an eighty-one-year-old man from Sun City, Florida, was arrested for attempted murder after his wife, who suffers from Alzheimer's, was found inside their van in a store's parking lot nearly suffocated by a plastic bag that had been placed over her head. According to a November 15, 2006, article in the *Tampa Tribune*, when police approached Meana in the store, he seemed unfazed and unconcerned by the news and continued shopping. He told his arresting officers that he'd had no intention of killing his wife—that he routinely, when his wife was feeling sick, put a plastic bag over her head so she wouldn't vomit on her clothes.

A twenty-three-year-old man needed to answer the call of nature, so he opened the passenger door of a pickup truck to urinate. Unfortunately, the truck was speeding down Houston's Southwest Freeway at the time and the man fell out and died when he was run over.

Source: *Houston Chronicle*, June 16, 2003

LOOK UNDER THE HOOD

Dominique Page was having difficulty steering her car, so she pulled into a gas station and looked under her car. The problem was so obvious, it was staring her right in the face. It was the body of forty-three-year-old Edison Fowler, whom Page had run over and dragged for nearly two miles. "The young woman was not the first person to hit him," said Detroit police sergeant Eren Stephens Bell. "He apparently was already a hit-and-run victim when she ran over him." According to the June 23, 2006, Associated Press article, no charges were expected against Page even though what she did was a real drag.

In a report from the South Carolina Public Safety Department, of the 122 pedestrians killed on the state's roads in 2006 "almost one-third" weren't actually "pedestrians" but were people "lying illegally in [the] road."

Source: Associated Press, January 1, 2007

MAY I HAVE YOUR ATTENTION, PLEASE

A January 25, 2001, Associated Press article reported that a twenty-five-year-old construction worker in Bethlehem, Pennsylvania, had grabbed his nail gun and fired a dozen nails into his head. Was it a botched suicide attempt? No. The man was trying to divert his attention from the excruciating pain brought on from having severed his hand in a miter saw accident just moments before. The man was rushed to a local hospital in stable condition and doctors performed the perfect manicure— they did his hands and nails.

"MOM FATALLY STABBED IN ARGUMENT OVER DISHES"

Atlanta Journal-Constitution headline, June 20, 2007

THE LETTER OF THE LAW

In New Zealand, there was a drop in the amount of posted mail being delivered and police soon found out the cause. On January 19, 2001, the *Otago Daily Times* reported that a forty-five-year-old man had pleaded guilty to stealing massive amounts of posted material over the previous four years because he was "lonely and liked reading other people's mail." Investigators found mail reaching a height of nearly three feet filling entire rooms of his house. Even though several envelopes contained checks, the man never tried to cash any—so it was deduced that he simply had a passion for reading.

"FROM HYENAS' PRIVATES, A POTENTIAL PUBLIC GOOD"

Contra Costa Times headline, May 27, 2003

WAS EMERY BORED?

On the morning of January 30, 2001, South Saint Paul, Minnesota, resident Emery S. Pluff kissed his wife good-bye and headed for work. But Emery didn't go to work; instead, he put on a Halloween mask and black cape that was kept in the family garage and reentered the house. He grabbed his wife and dragged her into the back room, where he molested and stole money from her, according to a February 2, 2001, article in the *St. Paul Pioneer Press*. She was more confused than frightened and, as she obviously knew who he was, continued asking her husband why he was doing what he was doing. To which he repeatedly replied, "I'm not Emery." After the robbery and assault, Emery did go to work—where police arrested him.

CRUEL and UNUSUAL
IDIOTS

(But True)

CRUEL AND UNUSUAL ∧ NEWSPAPER HEADLINES

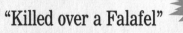

Volume IV

"Killed over a Falafel"

New York Post headline, October 29, 2006

///

"Man Builds Guillotine to Kill Himself"

Associated Press headline, September 12, 2007

///

"Student Runs over Driver's Ed Teacher"

Associated Press headline, February 12, 2005

///

"Spat over Horse Manure Wafts into Court"

Associated Press headline, September 14, 2007

///

"Fatal Tour Boat Unsafe"

Albany (NY) Times Union headline, July 26, 2006

///

"Dangerous Chemical Found in Women's Breasts"

San Francisco Chronicle headline, March 12, 2003

HABEAS CORPUS

Debby Messer of Livonia, Michigan, was threatened and harassed by her ex-husband, Gordie Milner, after their divorce, so she decided to file a $1 million lawsuit against him. Messer claimed she lives in fear and cannot stop feeling that he's stalking her—even though he died six months earlier. The February 5, 2001, article from the Associated Press reported that Messer is well aware her husband is dead but filed the suit claiming that Milner still "continue[s] to hurt me [and] hurt the children." To verify that Mr. Milner's estate has enough assets to pay in case she wins the suit, the court will have to check the "tax return of the living dead."

CRUEL and UNUSUAL IDIOTS

BRIDGING THE GAP

Neville Kan, a dentist in Chiswick, England, was acquitted of professional misconduct after being accused of drilling a hole in a patient's tooth and refusing to fill it until the patient paid the £35 she still owed. According to a July 18, 2003, article in the *Daily Telegraph* (London), the victim, identified as Mrs. B, claimed Kan told her, "Nothing lasts forever, I am not going to last forever . . . nothing in life is free. You owe me money." Even if the dentist was acquitted, he'll never receive a plaque for that kind of behavior.

MARK MY WORDS

"**S**ticks and stones can break my bones but names can never hurt me," didn't ring true to a Bluffton, South Carolina, man after his wife bit him over a few words. The words, however, according to Beaufort County sheriff's deputies, weren't spoken in love—they were scrawled over her body while she slept. The unnamed woman woke up on June 7, 2007, to discover that her husband, for reasons unknown, had written profanities on her arms, legs, and back with a pen. To his surprise, his wife added her own punctuation by puncturing his stomach with her teeth—possibly with the hope of removing his dangling participle.

AN IN-LAW AND AN OUTLAW

When Richard J. Kouns heard that his daughter and her husband had gotten into a fight, he told them he was coming over to their house to avenge his daughter. According to police reports, quoted in the June 15, 2001, edition of the *Ashland (KY) Daily Independent*, when Kouns arrived he was met by his son-in-law, Clark Schneeberger, who was fully prepared for battle. Clark had donned body armor and was poised with brass knuckles and a bayonet, when Kouns charged into the house swinging. The fight ended when Schneeberger bit off part of Kouns's nose—I guess he deserved it for being a nosy father-in-law.

"SON GETS SIX MONTHS, PROBATION, FOR DISMEMBERING MOTHER"

Associated Press headline, January 22, 2007

A HOUSE PET THAT GOT RATTLED

Michael Dean Messer of Waynesville, North Carolina, was taking one of his pets out for a stroll because Messer was worried after his "dog got him upset." In an article in the August 17, 2001, *Asheville Citizen-Times*, the pet that was taken outside "for some exercise" was a four-foot-long timber rattlesnake. Messer reported that he was "worried about him (not) eating," so he charmed the snake into eating a hen's egg. Going against the rule that says you shouldn't bite the hand that feeds you, the snake bit him.

CRUEL *and* UNUSUAL IDIOTS

"What are you going to do, stab me?"
asked Jackson Thomas of Brooklyn, New York,
shortly before being stabbed to death by his wife
after he had made derogatory comments
about her recent weight gain.

Source: *New York Post*, May 12, 2003

A Rose
by Any Other Name . . .

∽ PART III ∽

Arrested for exposing himself in the front window
of a Nashua, New Hampshire, business:
Mr. Joseph Dangle.

Nashua Telegraph, December 15, 2000

• • •

Suing the Oklahoma University law school
for unlawful expulsion:
Mr. Perry Mason.

Norman Transcript, January 11, 2001

• • •

Pleaded guilty of bank fraud in
Pine Ridge Oglala Sioux reservation, South Dakota:
Manuel Fool Head and his wife, **Sandra Fool Head**.

Sioux Falls Argus Leader–Associated Press, July 12, 2001

• • •

Booked for aggravated assault and burglary
in Salt Lake City, Utah:
Mr. Joe Snot.

CrimeReports.com, January 1, 2002

DID YOU SAY, "SUPREMACY"?

Richard Girnt Butler, founder of the white supremacy organization Aryan Nations, was kicked out of office for allegedly giving the organization a black eye and for routinely "surround[ing] himself with idiots." A *Philadelphia Daily News* article from January 29, 2002, recounted the events: In September 2000, Butler was forced to sell the group's twenty-acre Hayden, Idaho, compound after being sued by two Native Americans who were being harassed by the group. Victoria and Jason Keenan were driving past the compound when their car backfired; believing the noise to be the beginning of a government siege (like the 1993 Waco siege), some members of Aryan Nations shot at the car. The Keenans, who weren't hurt, sued Aryan Nations and won $6.3 million—thus forcing Butler to sell the group's compound. At least the skinheads weren't skinflints.

REWOUND TOO TIGHTLY

An ambulance was called after Bryan Allison fell twenty feet to the ground from the second-story balcony of his home in Buffalo, New York. While he was being examined in the hospital, Allison explained how the accident had come about. According to a *Buffalo News* article from November 19, 2001, Allison said he had been watching a videotape of a 1989 National Hockey League playoff game with his brother and gotten so angry after seeing his team lose again, some twelve years later, that he'd grabbed the television and tried to throw it out the window. Unfortunately, Allison had forgotten one small quirk in physics: that a falling object, if not released, will take with it the person who threw it.

"WHY MY BRAIN HATES YOUR MISTAKES"

Reuters headline, April 26, 2004

QUEEN OF THE HILL

Tacoma, Washington, resident Margaret Bobo helped take care of her ailing eighty-one-year-old mother, bringing her food and water every day. But apparently Bobo wasn't very good at tidying up around the house. According to an article in the January 20, 2002, edition of the *Spokane Spokesman-Review*, Bobo's mother was found living on top of a trash pile nearly four feet high inside a house overflowing with garbage. Bobo was arrested in January and admitted that she had never notified authorities about her mother or the trashed house, even though she confessed that it was difficult climbing over the huge pile of garbage to get to her mother and then having to slide back down to get out of the room.

Charged with stealing tires in Wilkes-Barre, Pennsylvania:
Edgar Spencer; his son, Edgar Spencer (Jr.);
the older man's brother, Edgar (W.) Spencer;
and his son, Edgar (W.) Spencer (Jr.).

Source: *Wilkes-Barre Times Leader*, May 8, 2002

THE FINALE RACK

The *Los Angeles Times* reported on February 24, 2003, that thirty-three-year-old Luis Chavez was arrested at his Cypress, California, condominium after he, for reasons unknown, deliberately set off aerial fireworks in his bedroom—resulting in $135,000 in damages. And two years later, for reasons known (he had consumed ten beers in rapid succession), thirty-eight-year-old Steven Glenn of Plainfield, Illinois, set off a ten-inch commercial fireworks shell in the living room of a house he was renting. "The whole house is pretty much, from the concussion of the explosion and the fire and the smoke, totaled," said Plainfield fire chief John Eichelberger. In the May 3, 2005, report from WMAQ-TV (Chicago), Glenn was treated and released but his girlfriend, Shauna Adams, required hospitalization.

SILENT BUT DEADLY

Ricki Stanley and Damian Jackson were working on Stanley's Ute automobile when they accidentally ruptured a propane tank and couldn't shut off the gas. Instead of trying to seal the leak, the two Hallam Victoria, Australia, men decided to go into Stanley's house for a small coffee. While they were waiting for the water to boil, gas filled the basement and, before the kettle whistled, the house exploded. It is estimated that the house was lifted a full six inches off its foundation, according to the June 6, 2005, article in the *Herald Sun* (Melbourne), and sustained nearly $400,000 in damages. Stanley said, "I'm never touching it again. It's taken everything away." Well, it didn't exactly take everything away or Stanley and his friend wouldn't be around to tell the tale.

A NEW LEASE ON LIFE

Dorothea Thomas let her ex-boyfriend into her Jacksonville, North Carolina, apartment and before she knew it, he'd pulled a gun, knocked her down, and shot her six times. Thomas miraculously survived the attack but broke her foot after she jumped from her second-story balcony to escape. According to a July 1, 2005, article in the *Jacksonville Daily News*, the day after Thomas returned home from the hospital, she found an eviction notice on her door. The district manager of United Dominion Residential Community, Peggy Piche, said Thomas had violated the terms of her lease because she was, among other things, too loud. Thomas had apparently breached the "six shots and you're out" rule.

CRUEL and UNUSUAL IDIOTS

Two men from Melbourne, Australia,
were reenacting scenes from their favorite movies.
One man portrayed Al Pacino's character in
Scarface, and the other man obliged and
accidentally shot him dead during the role-playing.

Source: *The Australian*, July 5, 2002

HOLY CRAP, BATMAN!

Police responded to an emergency call about a home invasion in the Singletree subdivision in Edwards, Colorado, but the call didn't come through the Bat-phone in Commissioner Gordon's office, which is unusual because the trespasser was Batman. According to an August 1, 2005, article in the *Vail Daily*, a fourteen-year-old boy dressed as the masked crusader entered a home through an unlocked door and was then chased and apprehended by the owner of the house and his son. "He believes he's on a mission to help people get off drugs," Kim Andree, spokeswoman for the sheriff's office, said. "He really believes he's helping. I think the family is working on getting him some assistance." Chief O'Hara tried to reach Alfred the Butler and Aunt Harriet, but both were unavailable for comment.

THIS CAR COMES FULLY EQUIPPED

A man purchased an abandoned car at a sheriff's auction in Brooklyn, New York, went about other business, and returned the following Monday to pick up his new purchase. While looking over his car, the man noticed a foul odor coming from the trunk. Since he had the keys, he popped open the trunk and quickly discovered the source of the smell—a dead man tied up with rope, handcuffed, wrapped in garbage bags, and covered with a blanket. Knowing this wasn't standard equipment on his car, he turned the matter over to the police. What did their inquiry turn up? A spokeswoman for the city medical examiner, who conducted an autopsy, said she considered the case a homicide. There's no word if the man decided to keep the car—which is too bad; he knows it's got a roomy trunk.

Carlos Little, who was suffering from a head injury, was picked up by police in a Savannah, Georgia, housing complex. He told police he had received the wound during a street robbery but a witness later told authorities that Little wasn't telling the truth. It turns out that Little and another man had gotten into a fight as to which one was more "endowed."

MIDDLE-AGED MIDDLE AGER

Robert McClain, forty-two, of Royal Oak, Michigan, literally went medieval on police officers when they arrived at his home after he had fled the scene of an automobile accident. The police were met at the door by McClain, who held them at bay by brandishing a four-foot sword and who then ran to the basement as he was pursued. There, McClain put on a chain-mail vest and leather gauntlets and started swinging a giant wooden mallet. He taunted the officers by saying, "I have a thousand years of power." However, the officers had a Taser with a thousand *volts* of power that knocked McClain on his middle-aged butt. According to the police records posted on TheSmokingGun.com on August 5, 2005, McClain was arrested and charged with felony assault and leaving the scene of an accident. No word on whether he was charged with misdemeanor geek.

WANNAHOCKALOOGIE

"It's certainly not prudent to open your car door on a highway," said Kansas City police spokesman Captain Rich Lockhart. "Especially when you're not wearing a seat belt." The captain was talking about the strange case of Robbin Doolin, who leaned out of her vehicle to spit on the road—and fell out. She went tumbling onto Highway 71 and, according to a July 31, 2005, article from the Associated Press, "hopped up and chased her car as it careened down an embankment." She was treated at a local hospital for injuries to her leg, arm, and head.

"TEEN GOLFERS CHARGED WITH GIVING THEIR TEAMMATE A WEDGIE"

USA Today headline, March 28, 2007

SCREAMING IN THE RAIN

The rain obviously clouded the judgment of one irate Los Angeles man after a pedestrian accidentally bumped into him near MacArthur Park. According to police, immediately after they collided the bumpee took his umbrella and jabbed it into the bumper's eye—and you thought opening an umbrella indoors is bad luck. The injured man was taken to a local hospital, where he was listed in stable condition even though it was discovered that the tip of the umbrella had lodged in his brain. The parasol-poking predator was never apprehended and some speculate it was actually Batman's archnemesis, the Penguin.

The name of the thirty-one-year-old man
from Land O' Lakes, Florida, charged on May 15, 2007,
with cultivating marijuana:

Robert Stoner.

A TUSSLE WITH TASSELS

When a customer at the Dream Girls Cabaret in San Diego, California, told stripper Lawanda Dixon that he didn't want a lap dance, she cut him. Not with a snide remark but with a knife. "He [Melik Jordan] said no," San Diego police detective Gary Hassen told Reuters on September 1, 2005. "She pulled a knife out of her bag and stabbed him." Even though police never found out why a topless dancer was carrying a bag, Dixon was arrested for assault with a deadly weapon and possession of methamphetamine.

"MALE INFERTILITY CAN BE PASSED ON TO CHILDREN"

Reuters headline, July 1, 2003

AS FUNNY AS A POKE IN THE EYE
WITH A SHARP STICK

Glenn Connolly called the Mercer, Pennsylvania, police and asked if they could contact his sister and let her know their mother had died. They duly conveyed the sad news to Victoria Christie, but soon found out a little more about the dearly departed—she wasn't dead. Connolly, for reasons unknown, thought it would be a funny gag to make his sister believe their mother had joined the choir invisible. But the joke is now on him, as he was arrested, according to a September 14, 2005, article in the *Chicago Sun-Times*, and fined $300 and ninety days in jail if convicted.

Cory McKinnon, of Arbour Glen Crescent, England, told his friend he was bored and needed "something to do." So the twenty-two-year-old attempted to scale down the side of his high-rise apartment complex, jumping from balcony to balcony. He lost his grip when he got back to his balcony and fell seven floors to his death.

Source: *National Post* (Canada), January 17, 2001

KILLSOMEONEFORME.COM

Eriko Kawaguchi of Tokyo, Japan, was so jealous that her lover's wife was pregnant that she went to the Internet and searched under "contract murder" to find someone to kill the woman. Kawaguchi contacted Takaharu Tabe, who promised to accomplish the dastardly deed. So is this just another case of someone hiring an undercover cop as a hired hit man and then being arrested? Nope. Kawaguchi was dissatisfied with the amount of time it was taking Tabe to murder the mother-to-be, so she went to the Tama Chuo police station to complain. She told officers she had already paid Tabe 15 million yen (U.S.$136,000) but he hadn't followed through with his end of the bargain. According to a September 14, 2005, article in the *Mainichi Daily News* (Japan), Kawaguchi was arrested and the pregnant woman was never harmed. I swear, if you can't trust a hit man at his word, whom can you trust?

ALL THE NEWS THAT'S FIT TO STEAL

Christopher M. Cooper approached a newspaper carrier in Jacksonville, Florida and told the man he had forgotten to deliver his newspaper. When the carrier asked Cooper for his address, he pulled out a pistol and shouted, "Give me a paper!" The carrier did just that and then contacted police who, according to the October 20, 2005, edition of the *Jacksonville Times-Union*, found Cooper at a gas station with a gun in his car and marijuana in his pocket. He was arrested and charged with armed robbery of the fifty-cent paper and possession of marijuana. Seems like he already had the pot, he just needed the paper.

"MAN CHARGED WITH BITING WIFE AFTER SHE REFUSED TO COOK DINNER"

Associated Press headline, April 2, 2007

CALLING DR. SCHOLL'S

An unnamed Manitoba man was found dead in a room in the McLaren Hotel on Main Street in Winnipeg, Canada, and officials were baffled as to his cause of death. According to Jim Hull, spokesman for the chief medical examiner, the autopsy report from the September 1998 incident concluded that the man "choked to death after biting calluses off his feet," illustrating the deadly side of putting one's foot in one's mouth.

CRUEL and UNUSUAL IDIOTS

"A woman, who told Roswell Police she had been on another planet for three years, reported a robbery Friday. She said a known person had taken the upper plate of her dentures valued at $800, silverware in a wooden box valued at $1,000, and various jewelry worth $1,000. She said she hadn't actually seen the named suspect take the items, but he 'moves so swift you can't see him.'"

Source: *Roswell (NM) Daily Record*, May 29, 2001

CRUEL *and* UNUSUAL IDIOTS

GET THEE TO A NUNNERY

A security guard at the World Famous Mustang Ranch, the notorious house of prostitution recently reopened and moved to Patrick, Nevada, heard the cries of a child in the parking lot and went to investigate. He found a two-year-old girl all alone in one of the cars, brought her inside, and called the local sheriff. It was estimated by deputies that the girl had been left inside the hot vehicle for nearly two hours—with temperatures in the car reaching 95 degrees. She was taken to a local hospital and treated for dehydration. According to an article in the September 4, 2007, edition of the *Reno Gazette-Journal*, when the girl's father, Lucien Hoffman of Bend, Oregon, finally left the house of ill repute, he was arrested on charges of child neglect.

DRIVEN TO DISTRACTION

A toll taker noticed ninety-three-year-old Ralph Parker's car as it approached the bridge and thought he was playing a Halloween prank—but it was no dummy sticking through the windshield, it was the body of a fifty-two-year-old man. Parker told police he hadn't even noticed the man who was halfway into his front seat. It must have "fallen out of the sky," Parker was quoted as saying in the October 21, 2005, edition of the *St. Petersburg (FL) Times*. The officers took Parker's driver's license, which was still valid for five more years, and asked the motor vehicle department to revoke it.

YOU'LL BREAK MY SPINE

"This bookstore is hard to find," said retired University of Minnesota librarian Carol Urness. "And once you get here, it's almost impossible to buy anything." Urness was quoted in a March 1, 2002, *Minneapolis Star Tribune* article about her new used book store in Saint Anthony, Minnesota, which consists of about one thousand books, all from her own collection. She stated that she rarely sells a book, not because of its location, but because she can't stand to part with any of them.

"The first day, a woman walked in and bought three books," she said, "and I about had a stroke." If she cries over each book, it would be a real dewy decimal system.

A sixty-six-year-old woman from
Menlo Park, California, Mrs. Jessie Brockman,
was thwarted in her attempt to commit suicide—
she had a heart attack and died of natural causes
before she could pull the trigger.

Source: Associated Press, September 27, 2003

I CAN'T BELIEVE IT'S NOT FROSTBUTTER

Calvert High School student Edward Lawrence Frostbutter was arrested in Calvert County, Maryland, and charged with raping a schoolmate in a restroom stall. But Frostbutter insisted he was innocent and claimed it was his alter ego "Sam" who sexually violated the young woman. According to a February 1, 2002, article in the *Washington Post*, Frostbutter stated that the girl knew about him and "Sam," and that she had gone into the bathroom stall voluntarily but acted surprised when "Sam" showed up and raped her. "Not in a box. Not with a fox. I do not like green eggs and ham. I do not like them Sam I am."

Frostbutter made the news after he was released from serving sixteen months in jail for sexual assault—when he was arrested for the murder of a fourteen-year-old girl. Hopefully some very large cell mate will frost Frostbutter's butt.

A FAMILY AFFAIR

Duane Perry was spreading the news that his ex-stepson, Jamie Ovitt, and Ovitt's mother, Debra, were both fathered by the same man, "Hebe" Ovitt, Jamie's grandfather and Debra's father. And although the charge was true, Jamie killed Perry. According to an article in the February 15, 2002, *Lebanon (NH) Valley News*, the murder didn't go very smoothly. Ovitt shot Perry but the bullet went through his body and hit Debra, who was assisting with the killing, on the knee. The couple then buried Perry on the family farm and, when they got into Perry's truck to make their getaway, they discovered the keys were still in the buried man's pocket.

A twenty-one-year-old man from Simcoe, Ontario, was charged in August 1998 with assault after he stabbed a fellow fisherman. Rawle Trotman was arrested after a violent argument over . . . a worm.

CRUEL *and* UNUSUAL IDIOTS

DUCT TAPE AND DUCTWORK

Lawrence Omansky's lawyer was quoted as saying, "The case will ultimately be viewed as a business dispute." But that description will also be in dispute. According to a *New York Times* article from April 18, 2003, a man named Schlosser had criticized Omansky's dealings as a property manager during a meeting in Omansky's office in the TriBeCa section of Manhattan. Omansky not only wanted to put Schlosser's comments under wraps, he wanted to put Schlosser under wraps, too—so he bound him with tape and jammed him into a three-foot-high crawl space under the second floor. After twenty-eight hours Schlosser was finally able to untape himself and escape. You can bet that Omansky's lawyer tried to tie up the court proceedings with a lot of red tape, too.

CRUEL *and* UNUSUAL
IDIOTS

IF THIS TRAILER'S ROCKIN' . . .

While working at Merial, Ltd., an animal vaccine manufacturing firm in Athens, Georgia, Nancy Fortson Reynolds embezzled more than $1 million—but she was finally caught and arrested and pleaded guilty to the charges. According to a May 28, 2003, article in the *Athens Banner-Herald*, a police detective reported that Reynolds and her husband, Larry, blew all of the money on an abundance of big-ticket consumer products (jewelry, motorcycles, electric guitars), but did make one strategic investment: they constructed an addition onto their double-wide mobile home. Larry, who at the time was a communications supervisor for the Oconee County Sheriff's Office, obviously hadn't asked how they could afford it.

A forty-three-year-old man in
Salt Lake City, Utah, was charged with
the kidnapping and abuse of his wife,
following an argument about
whether to attend church.

Source: *Salt Lake Tribune*, September 19, 2002

BOYS DON'T CRY

The *London Free Press*, in an article from May 17, 2003, told of the strange story of battered wife Elizabeth Rudavsky, who was charged with the stabbing death of her severely abusive husband, Angelo Heddington. Rudavsky had been married for only seven months but apparently had never noticed that Heddington was missing something. Was it compassion? The ability to control himself? No. It was a penis. Heddington wasn't a man at all. He, or she, was a woman. A former Heddington girlfriend who knew his/her secret told a reporter, "[Heddington] had soft hands, but she spit like a guy. The whole time you were talking to her, she'd have her hands in her pockets, playing with herself like she was a guy."

"MAN STOLE VIRGIN MARY STATUE FROM CEMETERY, PAINTED IT LIKE CLOWN"

USA Today headline, March 28, 2007

CRUEL *and* UNUSUAL IDIOTS

WHERE'S KING SOLOMON
WHEN YOU NEED HIM?

Police in Norcross, Georgia, arrested Khalidan Tunkara and Olin Washington, the parents of a nine-month-old baby girl. According to an April 12, 2003, article in the *Atlanta Journal-Constitution*, following an argument one of the parents sat the baby on the ground and drove away in an attempt to get the other parent to take the child—but that parent also drove away, leaving the baby stranded alone in the parking lot.

In a similar case, the *Chicago Tribune* reported in February 15, 2003, that a three-week-old girl was found by police in the street in front of a beauty salon in Elgin, Illinois, after her parents had left her there following an argument.

AN ALIEN CONCEPT

Robert Brayman was arrested in Westerly, Rhode Island, and charged with commanding Hobart Livingston to construct a pipe bomb he intended to use to kill a woman he was stalking. According to an article in the *Westerly Sun* from July 26, 2003, Livingston allowed Brayman total control over him, as he believed Brayman to possess supernatural powers. Over a three-year period, Livingston paid Brayman more than $13,000 for the spiritual protection of actress Natalie Portman, whom he believed was in danger from alien eggs that had been implanted in her—and which only Brayman could stop from hatching.

CRUEL *and* UNUSUAL
IDIOTS

"It isn't easy, but God said to [beat them],"
said former nun Lucille Poulin before her
sentencing for the callous discipline of children
under her care at her commune in
Charlottetown, Prince Edward Island, Canada.

Source: *Globe and Mail* (Toronto), September 30, 2002

HE SURE HAD SPUNK

"For almost 20 years," wrote a *Boston Globe* reporter in an article from March 24, 2002, "convicted rapist Benjamin LaGuer [incarcerated at the Massachusetts Correctional Institution at Norfolk] has waged a public campaign maintaining his innocence." LaGuer is serving time for the sexual attack of an elderly woman but has a group of supporters who believe in his innocence. Those supporters raised $30,000 for a DNA test in hopes of once and for all proving that LaGuer didn't perpetrate the crime. On March 22, the DNA test conclusively proved that the sperm found on the victim—was LaGuer's. C'est la Guerre!

In a similar case, Marshall Thomas, who was charged in 1999 with rape in Belleville, Illinois, demanded and received a DNA test he knew would make the prosecutor drop all charges. According to a February 15, 2002, article in the *Belleville News-Democrat* the results of the DNA matched an earlier, unsolved rape, and the 1999 rape case is still pending.

BLOOD MONEY

The Associated Press reported on March 22, 2002, that pharmacist Corey Penner of Newton, Kansas, pleaded guilty to sixteen counts of misdemeanor battery for his bizarre obsession of coercing people on the street to allow him to take a blood sample. Penner told his lawyer, who then told the court, that he's been drawing strangers' blood for the past eleven years and doesn't know why he feels compelled to do so. He also confessed that he gets people to submit to the blood draw by telling them he's conducting experiments or by simply offering them money.

A taste test turned violent in Pomona, California, when James Howle and Kevin Williams stabbed each other in a disagreement over which of their two alcoholic drinks tasted better.

Source: KNBC-TV (Los Angeles), October 21, 2003

THE PARTY WAS A REAL BLAST

J erry Stromyer of Wheeling, West Virginia, was dying to be the life of the party—and almost got his wish: the dying part, that is. A party-goer had tried unsuccessfully to make a blasting cap explode, when Stromyer took center stage, getting everyone's attention with the famous line, "Hey, watch this!" Stromyer placed the blasting cap in his mouth and bit down firmly—the March 18, 1986, explosion blew off his lips, teeth, and tongue. I'm sure one smart-ass in the crowd said, "That Stromyer, he's always shooting off his mouth."

Wood Dale, Illinois, native Pamela Majdan was charged with domestic battery on Memorial Day 2006 after repeatedly beating her sister, Joyce, during a quarrel. The argument centered around which sister had caught the most pieces of candy tossed during the town's holiday parade.

Source: *Arlington Heights (IL) Daily Herald*, May 31, 2006

ICH BIN EIN BERLINER

After receiving a free Krispy Kreme doughnut at a store promotion in Erie, Pennsylvania, a seventeen-year-old boy jumped back in line and asked for another doughnut, but he was refused. He returned moments later with a McDonald's bag over his head, according to the August 25, 2003, edition of the *Erie Times-News*, and demanded another doughnut, but was thwarted again. After this second rejection, the boy fell to the floor and began thrashing his arms and legs about, screaming for another doughnut, and was cited for disorderly conduct.

CRUEL and UNUSUAL IDIOTS

The stepfather of an eight-year-old boy
admitted to a very shocking form of discipline.
Child welfare officials removed the boy
from the house after the man brazenly admitted
using a stun gun on the child as punishment
for being late for school.

Source: *Houston Chronicle*, September 26, 2002

CRUEL *and* UNUSUAL
IDIOTS

SPIT OR SWALLOW?

Two men were arguing over a parking space at a Wilson, Wyoming, Kmart, according to an August 20, 2003, article in the *Jackson Hole News & Guide*, when one of the men spat at the other. As stated in the police report: "As [the victim] saw the projected body fluid traveling through the air, he dropped his jaw in shock, and the phlegm landed square in [his] mouth where he swallowed it in a gag reflex."

"PRIEST SAYS WOMAN WHO SELLS SEX TOYS CAN'T LEAD CHOIR"

Milwaukee Journal Sentinel headline, May 29, 2007

WHAT IN TAR-NATION!!!

Strange things happen in hotels and motels, but few are stranger than what happened at the Sandwich Motor Lodge in Massachusetts on November 11, 2003—and police are still baffled. A week earlier, the owners had complained that Daniel L. Kelleher, a carpenter, had left tar in the bathroom of a rented room. But things got really odd when Kelleher returned to the same room and was discovered by police covered from head to toe in roofing tar and lying in a water-filled bathtub. According to an article in Cape Cod's *Mashpee Enterprise*, Kelleher had apparently purchased the tar and caulking guns but, as to what happened after that, he is keeping mum. Whatever the reason, it's bound to be a sticky situation.

Police arrested and later released forty-three-year-old Gilbert D. Walker of Panama City, Florida, for breaking into a neighbor's home and chasing the occupant while wielding a dagger. Walker admitted he had acted crazy but blamed his actions on the fact that he had drunk too much jasmine tea.

Source: *St. Petersburg Times*, July 12, 2003

BEHAVIORAL PROBLEMS

Police officers Shawn Burger and Curt Charles of the Milwaukee, Wisconsin, police department were assisting other officers at the scene of a car accident when eighteen-year-old Thomas Smith began yelling obscenities and racial comments at them. When Burger and Charles walked over to confront Smith, he ran into his house and slammed the door. According to a December 27, 2004, article in the *Milwaukee Journal Sentinel*, Smith's mother, seeing what was going on, "said she didn't need that in her house," and shoved him back outside and into the arms of the two policemen. Smith fought with them, cutting one officer on the face, and broke free, but was captured a half-block away. After he was questioned by detectives, he wrote an apology letter to the two officers.

"NO CLEAR REASON FOR LACK OF MURDERS"

Athens (GA) Banner-Herald headline, June 9, 2007

. . . AND LEAVE THE DRIVING TO US!

A ntonio Hernandez pleaded guilty in Salt Lake City, according to a December 17, 2004, Associated Press article, of hijacking a Greyhound bus, en route from Los Angeles to Chicago, that had just left Green River, Utah. Hernandez took control of the bus after allegedly attacking the bus driver with a knife but was stopped about sixty miles later. He said that, had he not been stopped by police, he would have continued driving the bus with the intention of crashing it into his wife's trailer—five hundred miles away in Lexington, Nebraska.

CRUEL and UNUSUAL IDIOTS

An unidentified man in Panama City, Florida,
took one look at Amanda Hicks's baby and did
the dumbest thing in his life—he made fun
of the way the child looked. The twenty-year-old mom
and two of her girlfriends jumped into action
and punched, kicked, kneed, stripped, and burned
the man, and then sodomized him with
two different objects.

Source: *Panama City News-Herald*, December 25, 2002

A Rose
by Any Other Name . . .

⌐ PART IV ⌐

Arrested in West Haven, Connecticut, for spitting on a
police officer and urinating in his patrol car:
Ms. Lonna Leak.

New Haven Register, September 20, 2000

• • •

Sentenced to sixty years in prison for the
first-degree murder of a waitress in Washington, D.C.:
Gene Satan Downing.

Washington Times, December 5, 2001

• • •

Arrested on suspicion of embezzling more than $293,000
from the Locust Valley (New York) Cemetery Association:
Donald Death Jr.

Glen Cove Record-Pilot, April 24, 2005

• • •

Arrested for aggravated assault in Kingsport, Tennessee:
Mr. Innocent Safari Nzamubereka.

Kingsport Times-News, October 25, 2001

A BAD REFLECTION ON YOU

Floyd Elliot of Independence, Missouri, told police that, on December 14, 2004, he was viciously attacked in his apartment complex parking lot, stabbed in the stomach, branded with a hot knife, and had the word *fag* carved onto his forehead. According to a December 27, 2004, KMBC-TV (Kansas City) report, investigators handling the case were suspicious because the carved slur was backward (as if made by someone looking in the mirror). Elliot admitted to filing a false report of a hate crime but said he did it to increase police presence in his neighborhood.

"FLYING BOWLING BALL BREAKS BONE IN WOMAN'S LEG"

Greensboro (GA) Herald-Journal headline, July 17, 2003

POLLY WANNA CRACKLE?

John Freiburger Jr. returned to his Bettendorf, Iowa, home in April 1998 and discovered he was a victim of a robbery. A camera and tape player had been stolen but something else was missing. Freiburger just couldn't figure out what it was until he saw smoke coming from the microwave. He opened the door and found his pet Senegal parrot, Winston, cooked. Two teenage boys admitted they had been in the house but claimed they had nothing to do with the bird. "This is sick. We considered him part of the family," said Freiburger, who had paid $500 for the parrot four months before the roasting. "There was a waiting list for the parrot," he said. "I got it because they thought I would give him a good home." I'm sure Freiburger did give the parrot a good home—unfortunately, the boys gave him a home on the range.

BUMPER BOUNCER

A high school student from Chesterton, Indiana, Michael Morris, was rushed to the hospital in May 2006 suffering a broken leg and arm after being struck by a car. The driver of the car was Morris's friend, who admitted he had deliberately run over his pal—not out of anger but because Morris had asked him to. The friend described Morris as an adrenaline junkie who thrived on risky stunts and wanted to experience what it was like to be run over by a car. But Morris confessed to the *Northwest Indiana Times* that his days of road-rash behavior were over: "I won't do this no more."

Robert E. Mays, an associate dean at the University of Southern Illinois, pleaded guilty to aggravated assault in June 2006. In March, Mays was involved in a traffic accident and, when a Good Samaritan came to his aid, Mays bit him on the leg.

JUST TRY TO PACE YOURSELF

In February 2005, James Allan Donalson of Harris County, Texas, claimed his mother had died because of a defective pacemaker and, to prove it, cut the device out of her chest with a kitchen knife. According to an MSNBC report on March 16, 2005, Donalson finally turned in the pacemaker to authorities who then dropped an evidence-tampering charge against him. "No one wants to prosecute someone whose mother just died," Harris County assistant district attorney Leslie LeGrand III said.

"I'm not going to pay you, and there is nothing you can do about it," said Kenneth Hill shortly before being killed with a tire iron by a taxi driver in West Hempstead, New York, after Hill skipped out on a $5 fare.

Source: *Newsday*, May 5, 2003

A DILLY OF A DOLLAR

An employee of a Danville, Kentucky, Dairy Queen really did get "something different" and caused a "Blizzard" of trouble when she accepted a $200 bill from a customer—and gave her $197.88 in change. The *Louisville Courier-Journal* reported on January 30, 2001, that the funny money featured a picture of George W. Bush and was so crudely made that the Secret Service said it would not file counterfeiting charges. They said it would be too difficult to prove to a jury that the bill could be confused with real money—even though they had proof that one dippy DQ employee had made the mistake.

"INDIAN TESTICLE ATTACK 'IS MURDER'"

BBC News headline, January 28, 2003

CRUEL and UNUSUAL IDIOTS

WE SAID READ *GOODNIGHT MOON*

Colleagues said they tolerated the bizarre behavior of a first grade teacher in Pine Grove Elementary School in Brooksville, Florida, for months but didn't have sufficient grounds to fire her until she finally cracked—by dropping her pants and mooning everyone at a staff meeting. According to a February 1, 2005, article in the *St. Petersburg Times*, Susan Bartlett was considered "out of control," was accused of smoking pot, "burped loudly" to disrupt staff meetings, and "yell[ed] at the kids all the time," using words like *butt* and *stupid*. After Bartlett literally showed her ass, she was ordered to take a drug test, which she refused, claiming there was a "lack of just cause." It was only after that, that the school board demanded her resignation. I'm not sure about you, but she sounds like a pretty fun teacher to me.

THREE LIMP NOODLES

On July 28, 2000, three fifteen-year-old boys were rushed to Duke Hospital in Durham, North Carolina, all suffering from gunshot wounds to the leg. After media speculation about the shootings, police reported that the boys confessed they had all voluntarily shot each other. A police spokesman was quoted as saying, "They wanted that status symbol of telling their friends they were shot." They wanted to be cool like 50 Cent, but they wound up looking like a bunch of plugged nickels.

CRUEL *and* UNUSUAL IDIOTS

"I don't care who f*@#ing died. I'm more important!" declared Anna Gitlin, after bumping a police officer with her car because she was frustrated that a rush-hour accident had blocked traffic in Weymouth, a suburb of Boston, Massachusetts.

Source: *Boston Globe*, June 25, 2003

POLICE COLLAR AND A DOG COLLAR

On February 26, 2004, a deputy tried to stop thirty-seven-year-old Girlamo Marinello of Shelby Township, Michigan, for running a stop sign in Oakland Township. Marinello rammed the deputy's car and then got out of his vehicle and started swinging—not his fists—but a four-pound French toy poodle on a leash. According to a January 17, 2005, article in the *Detroit Free Press*, Marinello was charged with animal cruelty, assault with intent to do great bodily harm, fleeing and eluding while causing a collision, and carrying concealed weapons (knives found in the truck—not the poodle). The state forensic psychiatry center found Marinello not criminally responsible and the poodle was put up for adoption.

"MAN STABBED AFTER ARGUMENT OVER ARGUMENTS"

Milwaukee Journal Sentinel headline, June 6, 2006

EVERYBODY CUT FOOTLOOSE

In a bizarre case of putting one foot in front of the other, police on Jedidiah Island, British Columbia, Canada, were a shoe-in for the most confused police force, when a human foot was found still wearing a sock and a size 12 sneaker. Six days later, on the nearby island of Gabriola, another foot, wearing a sock and a size 12 sneaker, was found on the beach. Odd? Yes. But odder still is the fact that they were both right feet and obviously didn't belong to the same person. "Finding one foot is like a million to one odds," confirms RCMP spokesman Corporal Garry Cox in an August 31, 2007, article in the *Sun* (Vancouver). "But to find two is crazy. I've heard of dancers with two left feet, but come on." Maybe the owners of the feet were just doing the Hokey Pokey and they turned themselves around.

SOMETHING SMELLS FISHY

A businesswoman from Harare, Zimbabwe, Magrate Mapfumo, was frantic after having her car and millions of Zimbabwean dollars (ZWD) stolen, so she sought the help of . . . a musician, Edna Chizema. Chizema, according to a March 17, 2005, Associated Press article, convinced Mapfumo to pay her thirty million ZWD to enlist the aid of enchanted mermaids who would help recoup the losses. Chizema said the money was to fly four mermaids in from London, England, put them up in a luxury hotel, and equip them with cell phones. Mapfumo was also told that she "could not see the mermaids as only spirit mediums could do so." When Chizema wanted to fly in an Arabian mermaid, Mapfumo became suspicious and alerted authorities. Chizema was charged with theft by false pretenses. No word on whether the mermaids were charged with any crime.

THIS IS A GREAT PLACE FOR A STICKUP

When someone we care about dies, it's very difficult to let go. But one Punta Gorda, Florida, man didn't let go of his dead eighty-six-year-old roommate for a different reason—he wanted to keep using his ATM card and cash his checks. David Morse, forty, was arrested after a rent collector stopped by, smelled a disgusting odor, and alerted the authorities. Morse said his roommate, John Jones, had died a month earlier of natural causes but that he hadn't called police because Morse had outstanding arrest warrants. An Associated Press article from September 28, 2007, reported that Morse took $2,000 from his decomposing roommate's bank account by means of ATM withdrawals and checks.

The author of the book *Understanding Stupidity* and the self-proclaimed authority on dumb decisions, James F. Welles, was arrested for soliciting sex on the Internet from a forty-year-old policeman posing as a fifteen-year-old girl.

Source: *Palm Beach Post*, November 8, 2002

THERE'S ALWAYS CIVIL SERVICE

The *Des Moines Register* reported in an article on March 25, 2005, that Barbara Dutton was denied unemployment benefits because, according to records cited by the administrative law judge, Dutton, who worked as a supply clerk at a twelve-person Des Moines company, ordered office supplies in excess of $230,000 during an eighteen-month period. Orders were placed for 16,000 Bic pens and approximately $15,000 worth of Scotch tape. The judge found no evidence of fraud by Dutton and could only conclude that she was simply incompetent.

"PROBE OF GAY CLERGYMAN ENDS"

Reuters headline, August 5, 2003

A CRUEL AND UNUSUAL EXPERIENCE

A young man from the village of Yangping in the city of Lingbao, Henan province, China, had an argument with his parents, ran away from home, and found refuge in an abandoned house in a gold-mining area near the village. He was found dead the next day, a victim of cyanide poisoning. According the Chinese news agency Xinhua, as reported in a September 28, 2007, report from Reuters, "As the crowd flocked in at the invitation of [the man's] parents, the floor of the house, made of a single wooden board over the pond, gave way and 16 people fell into the two-meter-deep chemical pool." The chemical pool to which the article referred was a pool of cyanide, used to extract gold from ore. Of the sixteen people, seven were saved and sent to local hospitals; the other nine died from cyanide poisoning or injuries.

YOU ARE GETTING SLEEEEEEPY

David Winniewicz was arrested in Chartiers Township, Pennsylvania, for allegedly using amateur sleep hypnosis to program his ten-year-old stepson to kill the boy's four-year-old brother. Winniewicz's wife found a cassette tape of the subliminal messages Winniewicz played to the boy while he slept and turned it over to authorities. According to an article in the *Washington (PA) Reporter-Observer*, on January 22, 2004, the tape included Winniewicz's suggesting different ways to kill the younger boy (e.g., strangle him with your hands; put a pillow over his face). I have a feeling the messages Winniewicz's cellmate will give him won't be subliminal.

A prisoner in a Kingman, Arizona, jail accidentally died after he excreted on the floor of his cell and then later slipped on it and cracked his head on the floor.

Source: Associated Press, April 17, 2002

THIS IS YOUR BRAIN ON DRUGS

An article from the April 14, 2005, issue of the *Barre-Montpelier Times Argus* told of the story of seventeen-year-old Nickolas Buckalew of Morrisville, Vermont, who was charged with digging up a corpse. After Buckalew dug up the dead body on April 8, he hacked off the head and took it with him (it was later found near his home). Court documents report that Buckalew had bragged about stealing the head and told people that his intention was to make a bong out of it. On June 28, 2006, he was sentenced from one to seven years for the mutilation of the corpse. Had Buckalew succeeded in making the bong, it would have been an actual "pot head."

"MAN FINED FOR HIDING HIS SALAMI"

Australian Associated Press headline, January 16, 2005

A SERIES OF UNFORTUNATE EVENTS

Tim Brender "knew he needed to start getting things organized," said his wife, Lani, of their upcoming move. So the Madison, Wisconsin, man went down into the basement of his rented townhouse to start packing, He moved a table that knocked over a can of spray paint that fell on a hammer lying on the floor. The claw of the hammer punctured the spray paint can, which started spraying like an out-of-control garden hose. The can spun around and squirted paint on the pilot light of the hot water heater. The flame roared up and set fire to a cushion and quickly spread to a container of gunpowder. From there, things just got worse and eventually the fire consumed everything in the house. Lani was quoted in the April 9, 2005, edition of the *Madison Capital Times* as saying, "You couldn't set up this scenario to happen." To which I would say, "Why would you want to?"

A FLAGRANT FOUL

The coach of a youth basketball team playing in Fayetteville, Georgia, became more and more argumentative because of the "bad calls" of referee Oliver Lewis Wood. After the game, as reported in the February 14, 2001, edition of the *Atlanta Journal-Constitution*, the referee had had enough of the backbiting comments from the coach of the seven- and eight-year-old players so he took a knife and stabbed him. The coach, who was a county marshal, needed seventeen stitches and the referee, who was by day a Baptist minister, was arrested. And they say kids don't have any role models these days.

"PSYCHOPATHS COULD BE BEST FINANCIAL TRADERS—RESEARCH"

Reuters headline, September 19, 2005

A HEAD BY A FOOT

The Mini Warehouse Rentals in Maiden, North Carolina, auctioned off property forfeited by a renter who was delinquent paying his storage fee. Shannon Whisnant got a very good bargain on a meat smoker. However, according to an Associated Press article from September 27, 2007, the previous owner had left some meat in it—a human foot. John Wood, the former owner of both the smoker and the foot, said he'd lost his leg in a plane crash but wanted to keep it. As he explained, "I had some spiritual beliefs that I wanted to be cremated whole, so I had my leg preserved." Police promised Wood he will get his leg back—and Whisnant can keep the smoker if he wants.

ANOTHER SERIES
OF UNFORTUNATE EVENTS

The *Daily Telegraph* (London) of April 13, 2005, tells of the bizarre fatal automobile accident involving Alison Taylor and her Peugeot. The Peugeot wouldn't start, so Taylor pulled out a hammer to tap on the starter as it obviously had a dead spot and wouldn't turn over. She had done this before, but this time she left the keys in the ignition. When the starter engaged, the car sprang to life and, as she had also left the car in gear, it began rolling over her. As a reflex, she instinctively grabbed something —unfortunately, it was the throttle cable. The car accelerated, dragging Taylor with it, and eventually went over an embankment. The coroner in North Tyneside, England, declared the cause of Taylor's death an "accident."

CRUEL *and* **UNUSUAL IDIOTS**

Fred William Leigh was playing horseshoes
with a friend in Frederick, Maryland, when he
got a ringer. His opponent insisted it wasn't a ringer
and the argument escalated until Leigh pulled out
a .38 and shot the man in the stomach.

Source: *Frederick News Post*, December 10, 2002

A PAIN IN THE NECK

Christine Rivano was walking in the Massapequa Preserve watching her boyfriend playfully throwing a stick for his dog to retrieve. The boyfriend, who is a knife collector, pulled out a hunting knife and wanted to see if he could throw the stick and hit it with the knife. It stuck all right, but not in the stick; it stuck in Rivano's neck. According to an April 8, 2005, article in *Newsday*, Nassau police called the occurrence a "freak accident" and Rivano was taken to a hospital and put into a medically induced coma while doctors repaired her throat.

"FLIES ARE LIKE US: SCIENTISTS"

News Limited (Australia), July 8, 2003

A BONDED BOND

As Suzanne Editha Edwards was released on $1,000 bail and before she ever left the courthouse, she wanted to show her appreciation to her husband who had posted her bond. She ran to him and then punched him and scratched him repeatedly, and he retaliated by socking her a few times, too. According to an August 5, 2002, article in the *Longview (TX) News-Journal*, Ms. Edwards's bail was then increased to $10,000 and she was re-released later that day without incident. Her husband was then scheduled to stand trial for domestic abuse and attempting to run over a police officer.

In a cliché come to life, a twenty-nine-year-old man from Downers Grove, Illinois, decided to set off some fireworks in his yard (although it wasn't anywhere near the Fourth of July). When one of the rocket tubes didn't go off, he picked it up and looked into one end to see what was wrong— needless to say, he went out with a bang.

Source: *Chicago Tribune*, May 8, 2007

FULL METAL JACKASS

In another case of someone getting hurt by playing with live ammunition, a .22-caliber bullet wounded Chaddrick Dickson of Monroe, Louisiana, after he repeatedly slammed it on the ground. According to an article from the December 30, 2001, edition of the *Seattle Times*, Dickson claimed he wanted to remove the gunpowder from the casing because he planned to mix it into his dog's food to make the animal meaner.

"GIRL HEADED FOR EYE DOCTOR ENDS UP WITH TEETH PULLED INSTEAD"

KTRK-TV (Houston, TX) headline, March 31, 2003

HIGH PLAINS GRIFTER

An article in the August 15, 2002, edition of the *Fort Payne (AL) Times-Journal* highlighted Judith Lynn Ashmore, a woman who should be inducted into the grifter's hall of fame for a scam she pulled on a family of four. Ashmore flimflammed the family into accompanying her on a four-month, eight-state crime spree by convincing them that she needed help with her terminal cancer and then, after she played out that hand, conned them into believing she was in the witness protection plan. The only thing one can truly believe about Ashmore is that she was eventually found guilty of fraud in August 2002.

"ORANGE COUNTY MARKET WORKER STABBED IN ARGUMENT OVER STACKING CUCUMBERS"

Associated Press headline, September 13, 2007

YOU CAN'T TAKE IT WITH YOU

Larry Nettles, of Charleston, South Carolina, returned from the funeral home clutching a small pink plastic bag he was told contained his deceased father-in-law's personal effects. But the contents were more personal that Nettles ever thought. Days later, a pungent odor emitted from the closet and the real contents were discovered after the family cat clawed open the bag. "It was him in the bag, not his personal belongings," Nettles said. The funeral home had accidentally given him a medical waste bag used to hold the deceased's heart and other organs that are removed after an autopsy. He contacted the funeral home and was told to simply bury the contents in his backyard. But Nettles, having more guts than most people, threatened a lawsuit if the funeral home didn't give the organs a proper burial.

CRUEL *and* **UNUSUAL IDIOTS**

A forty-three-year-old man stopped at a red light
at an intersection in Lynwood, California, and waited
for it to turn green. The man was obviously a
very conscientious driver because, even though
there was no traffic coming and the light stayed red
for an unusually long time, he refused to run it.
The person in the car behind the law-abiding driver
began to turn redder than the light and pulled out a gun
and shot the reluctant driver dead.

Source: *San Jose Mercury News*, January 25, 2001

THE DECLINE OF MODERN CIVILIZATION

Violence has so permeated our society that we rarely look twice at, say, one student's attacking another student at school—unless, of course, both the attacker and the victim are five years old. According to an October 1, 2007, article in the *Daily Telegraph* (London), Junaid Judge suffered two small wounds after being attacked by a child wielding a thin craft blade. No criminal action can take place against the assailant as he is under the age of criminal responsibility, which is ten. He was, however, suspended for the day, kept away from the other children during school, not allowed out at break, and must now be taken home at lunch by his parents.

"TWO JAILED AFTER BRIDGE BUILT BY BLIND MAN COLLAPSES"

Reuters headline, June 11, 2007

YOU WANT FRIES WITH THAT?

Cleveland, Ohio, police arrested a thirty-year-old man and his eighteen-year-old accomplice after they attacked employees at a drive-through window at the Rally's restaurant on Snow Road. According to the employees, the two men pulled up to the window and sprayed a can of "Fart Spray" at them. As a precaution, the manager threw away $1,000 worth of food and had three employees go to the Southwest Medical Center to be checked out (or aired out). A September 25, 2007, Associated Press article quoted Steve Presser, the owner of Big Fun, a novelty store that sells the offensive spray: "You have to be careful. You have to know where you are doing it and who you are doing it to." Says Presser, "I feel sorry for them because this is an overwhelming smell."

MINIONS OF THE EVIL EMPIRE

A Butler, Pennsylvania, woman was sentenced to thirty to sixty years in prison for the cruel and unusual murder of a mentally disabled man. Melissa Adams pleaded guilty to third-degree murder in the death of thirty-year-old Jason Michael Ritzert, whose body was found burned beyond recognition and stuffed in a trash container. Ritzert was forced to wear a lighter-fluid-soaked-T-shirt and sit in a bath while Adams and two others set him on fire, because they thought Ritzert was stealing from them. After he lost consciousness, they continued beating on his body and finally put him in the trash bin and set fire to his body again. A September 27, 2007 article from the Associated Press reported that, at the sentencing, Adams asked Ritzert's family to forgive her.

"'GIGGLES THE CLOWN' IN COURT ON CHILD SEX CHARGES"

Associated Press headline, September 27, 2007

DOCTOR-PATIENT PRIVILEGES

Some doctors lack appropriate bedside manner, but this nationally recognized La Jolla, California, cardiologist beats everyone else to the punch. Dr. Maurice Buchbinder was accused of making "chopping like blows to the patient's abdomen," tried to hit his leg "with a substantial amount of force," and "used the tip of his elbow to hit [him] on the forehead," the *San Diego Union-Tribune* reported on September 26, 2007. The patient was placed on a gurney following angioplasty and was attacked by Buchbinder who yelled, "You are an animal" and then "grabbed and twisted the patient's nose," making it turn "bluish," witnesses told reporters. Scripps Memorial Hospital placed Buchbinder on indefinite suspension while it launched its own investigation.

THEY'RE REALLY STACKING THEM IN THERE

Sisters Marcelle Lieberman and Harriet Lieberman Mellow went to the Congregation Beth Israel synagogue to look after their mother's cremated remains but her ashes, which were supposed to be kept behind a locked glass door of her niche in the mausoleum, were gone. In their place, the sisters were shocked to find a can of sour-cream-and-onion potato chips. The sisters are suing the synagogue and two funeral companies for misplacing their mother's ashes, according to an Associated Press article from June 10, 2005. "To their added horror," the lawsuit states, "Harriet and Marcelle learned that the can had been visible in the niche for at least six months." I can just hear the comments, "Oh, my, Mr. Pringle—he looked so young."

CRUEL and UNUSUAL IDIOTS

Robert Carnathan was charged with beating a seventy-nine-year-old man to death in a conflict over collecting lost golf balls on a golf course in Quincy, Massachusetts. Carnathan routinely collected balls at the course and sold them back for a discount, and didn't want the other man barging in on his turf — the victim had only wanted a single golf ball to give to his grandson.

Source: *Boston Herald*, November 13, 2002

A REAL GENERAL GRIEVOUS

Mark Webb, twenty, and Shelley Mandiville, seventeen, of Hemel Hempstead, Hertfordshire, England, wanted to re-create the Lightsaber fight scene from the Star Wars film *Revenge of the Sith*. But as neither of them had the Lucas-style budget, they decided to improvise and took two fluorescent light tubes, filled them with gasoline and dishwashing liquid, and then it was "lights, camera, disaster." The tubes exploded, covering the two with the flaming mixture. According to a June 23, 2005, article in the *Sun* (UK), police found a video camera next to a badly burned area of ground and suspected that someone had been filming the stunt but had run when the two stars became two supernovas.

Arrested on charges of drug possession, driving while intoxicated, and driving without a license:

Mr. Fred Flintstone.

Source: *Lewisville (TX) Leader*, February 14, 2005

PIN IT ON THE JANITOR

Peter Flores, a maintenance man at the Gadsden Middle School in Anthony, New Mexico, had seen all sorts of weird things the kids have brought to school but this even surprised him—a hand grenade. So he did the most proper thing in a situation like this, according to a police investigator. "He pulled the [pin] because he was curious what would happen." According to an article in the *Las Cruces Sun-News* of June 24, 2005, the grenade turned out to be a tear-gas canister and it immediately began spewing CS gas that permeated the entire building. Flores was hospitalized with minor injuries. School officials say it's a "big mystery" where the canister came from. Fortunately, no students were in the building when Flores pulled the pin.

"STUFFED DUCK EXPLOSION ENDS BADLY"

Newton (MA) TAB headline, March 5, 2005

FIRST CLASS AND CERTIFIED IDIOTS

A mailman in Columbus, Ohio, asked the owner of a dog if she would please take the dog inside (because we all know the tenuous relationship between postmen and dogs, right?). Well, it wasn't the dog the mailman should have worried about, it was the woman's sixteen-year-old son who suddenly attacked the USPS man. The mail carrier retaliated by spraying the boy with a can of Mace, and that's when the boy's uncle joined in the fun. The uncle, George Cranshaw, threw a tire iron at the postal employee—but missed and hit his nephew. In a story from the May 24, 2003, edition of the *Columbus Dispatch*, Cranshaw was charged with negligent assault and attempted felonious assault, the teenage boy recovered from his wounds, and the mailman was congratulated for not "going postal" on the whole family.

Nineteen-year-old Raymond Garbaldon was
charged with breaking and entering a stranger's home
in Albuquerque, New Mexico, but not to steal anything.
Apparently Garbaldon only wanted to turn on an
outside light so he could see on the porch, where he
was in the process of shaving his friend's head
with a pair of electric clippers.

Source: *Albuquerque Journal*, February 27, 2001

AND THEN, I HIT HIM IN THE FIST WITH MY FACE

"That's the first time I messed up. A person who's not a bad person deserves a second chance," claimed Antonio Aragon during his trial for attempted murder in San Antonio, Texas. Jill Garza, a mother of three and former girlfriend of Aragon, spoke in his defense, saying that she still loved him: "It wasn't him that day," prosecutors "don't know him," and "He's not a violent person." Which are all interesting statements considering it was Garza whom Aragon nearly beat to death, repeatedly kicked and punched, and then ran over three times with his car. Garza explained away the brutal attack by saying Aragon's fury had been sparked when he'd locked himself out of his car and had to break a window to retrieve his keys. According to an article in the July 9, 2003, edition of the *San Antonio Express-News*, the jury found Aragon guilty anyway.

"They don't like each other. [The other girl] is a snot,
and my daughter can be a snot, too,"
said the mother of a Brainerd (MN) high school
sophomore cheerleader who was suspended
for allegedly offering $50 to have a
senior cheerleader beaten up.

Source: *Brainerd Dispatch*, October 30, 2003

THE ONE THAT GOT AWAY

A search team was sent out after James Brady and two of his buddies had gone fishing but not returned home. A television news helicopter located the boat, overturned, partly submerged but still anchored, and the bodies of Brady's friends were pulled from the water. More than a month and a half later, Brady's body popped up—not on Florida's west coast, where his boat had sunk, but on Florida's east coast—more than five hundred miles away. The body was identified because the victim's pager was still attached to his belt. A Coast Guard spokesman said the body simply must have traveled around the Florida peninsula during the time it was reported missing. No report on how many pages were beeped in during his voyage.

"BALD MAN ACCUSED IN HAIR-LOSS THEFT"

Associated Press headline, September 12, 2007

TRICK-OR-FREAK

On Halloween Night 2003, a forty-three-year-old man in Ann Arbor, Michigan, joyfully walked along while his son was trick-or-treating. After approaching one house, the young boy came running back to his father, crying because the homeowner hadn't given him any candy. The man stomped up to the storm door and demanded to know why the woman had stiffed his son. She said she had given the little boy candy, and the father-and-son team left the porch—only to return a few minutes later, when the man handed the woman a small note and told her to call the police. The police report from a November 3, 2003, Associated Press article states that the boy's father then threw a pumpkin through the woman's front window, smashed another against her front door, and ripped out and destroyed a bird feeder in her front yard. When police arrived at the man's home later that night, they weren't there to trick-or-treat.

KNOT NICE

Talk about getting your lines crossed: A Japanese man, Yoshinori Sato, agreed to a blind date with Hiromi Mikado, a woman who had called him at a telephone dating club, and they had arranged to meet in front of a cream puff store (not making this up, folks). They checked into a "Saitama love hotel" and Mikado asked if Sato was up for a little S&M—he agreed. Mikado blindfolded him and ordered him to lie facedown on the bed. She then reached under the bed and pulled out a nylon cord and strangled him to death. When she was arrested, she simply explained, "I don't know why he died," and later said, "I just wanted to kill somebody." In a little cruel irony, the incident was reported on Valentine's Day 2004 in the *Mainichi Daily News* (Japan).

THIRD TIME'S A CHARM

According to a July 5, 2007, Associated Press article, Tony Hicks of Knoxville, Tennessee, hit the hospital Trifecta for three separate wounds on three consecutive days: July 1—Hicks was hit by a car at night and released from the hospital the following morning. July 2—Hicks was attacked in his home by an intruder and released from the same hospital the next day. July 3—Hicks was shot by police in connection with a robbery, taken to the same hospital again, and released—into police custody.

An inmate at a psychiatric prison in Abbotsford, British Columbia, Canada, flew into a fierce frenzy and took his therapist hostage after fellow inmates made fun of his drawing of "toilet paper" during a game of Pictionary.

Source: *Vancouver Sun*, July 9, 2003

I LOVE EWE

An unnamed Wanaka, New Zealand, man contacted the police in the middle of the night to complain that a pregnant sheep was sleeping in the bed with him. When officers arrived, the sheep had already hoofed it and there were no traces of "wool or hoof marks in the bed." The complainant could not identify any distinguishing marks on the sheep, but the police didn't believe the man tried to pull the wool over their eyes. They told the man, who had admitted to being intoxicated the night before, that he was probably the victim of a prank—and to "give up the drink." An August 27, 2005, article from the New Zealand Press Association, stated that the police never inquired how the man knew the sheep was pregnant.

"AND YOU THOUGHT THE NUMBER 666 WAS BAD NEWS"

San Francisco Chronicle headline, February 23, 2007

CRUEL AND UNUSUAL (But True) NEWSPAPER HEADLINES

Volume V

Just in case you didn't get enough weird
headlines, I bring you the final installment.

"Indian Lawyers Tie Man to Tree, Beat Him"

Reuters headline, May 31, 2007

///

"Woman Gets Probation for Chasing Kids with Dildo"

Pottstown (PA) Mercury, headline, October 20, 2003

///

"Principal Admits Throwing Excrement"

Star (Toronto) headline, April 2, 2007

///

"Cops: Man Put Dog Feces in Envelope with Parking Ticket"

USA Today, May 8, 2007

///

"Palm Beach County Man Arrested for Making False Teeth without a License"

South Florida Sun-Sentinel headline, April 24, 2007